KITCHEN TABLE

100 Great Chicken Recipes

AINSLEY HARRIOTT

www.mykitchentable.co.uk

Welcome to my KITCHEN TABLE

You can create a wonderful variety of dishes with the humble chicken, and I've collected **100 of my favourite roasts, bakes, soups, stir-fries, grills and stews**, plus some special treats that are perfect for sharing with friends.

Contents

Chicken and Sweetcorn Soup

A popular soup, traditionally from the southwest of China. It's delicious, easy to make and thoroughly heart-warming. You can also try making it with a tin of creamed sweetcorn – if so, leave out the cornflour, as the soup is already quite thick.

Step one Heat the oil in a deep pan and gently cook the chicken, garlic and ginger for 3–4 minutes without colouring.

Step two Blend the cornflour with a little stock and add to the soup pan with the remaining stock and the sweetcorn. Bring to the boil, stirring continuously, and simmer gently for 5–7 minutes.

Step three Beat together the egg and lemon juice and slowly trickle this into the soup pan, stirring with a chopstick or fork to make egg strands. Season to taste, garnish with the salad onions and toasted sesame seeds, and serve with a drizzle of soy sauce and some prawn crackers.

Serves 2

1 tbsp vegetable oil

100g (4oz) boneless, skinless chicken breast, finely diced

1 garlic clove, finely chopped

1cm (½ in) piece of fresh root ginger, finely chopped

1 tbsp cornflour

600ml (1 pint) hot chicken stock

100g (4oz) sweetcorn kernels, thawed if frozen

1 egg

1 tbsp fresh lemon juice

Salt and freshly ground black pepper

shredded salad onions, to garnish

toasted sesame seeds, to garnish

dark soy sauce and prawn crackers, to serve

Hot and Sour Chicken and Mushroom Soup

Hot and sour soups are delicious. My recipe is made with chicken, but you could also try making it with prawns, diced or minced pork, or just extra vegetables. Look out for frozen wontons and fish wontons in oriental stores or good supermarkets – the wontons make a great addition to the soup.

Serves 2

1 stick lemon grass

600ml (1 pint) hot chicken stock

4 boneless, skinless chicken thighs, diced

1–2 tsp Thai red curry paste

1 shallot, finely chopped

100g (4oz) shiitake mushrooms, sliced, or canned straw mushrooms, halved

2 tsp light muscovado sugar

2 tsp fish sauce

juice of 1 lemon

1 salad onion, thinly sliced

1 red chilli, thinly sliced

handful of fresh coriander leaves

salt and freshly ground black pepper

Step one Flatten the lemon grass with a rolling pin or meat mallet and place in a pan with the chicken stock, chicken, curry paste and shallot; bring to the boil.

Step two Add the mushrooms to the pan and simmer gently for 8–10 minutes.

Step three Stir the sugar and fish sauce into the soup and simmer for 3 minutes until the chicken is cooked. Squeeze in the lemon juice and season to taste.

Step four Ladle the soup into bowls and scatter over the salad onion, chilli and coriander. Serve immediately.

If any of my family are feeling a bit off-colour, I throw lots of shredded root ginger into the broth for a really soothing soup – especially good for coughs and colds.

Shredded Chicken and Lemon Grass Soup

This is a low-fat, delicate, aromatic broth. It makes a lovely light supper or can serve up to six as a starter. For this soup I use the whole chilli, including the seeds, which, when blended with the other flavours, gives the soup a wonderful kick. Make sure you use whole thighs with the bones in as they contribute greatly to the flavour of the broth.

Serves 4

6 whole chicken thighs

2 sticks lemon grass

2 kaffir lime leaves

2 garlic cloves, halved

1 red chilli, roughly chopped

4cm (1½ in) piece of fresh root ginger, thickly sliced

1.5 litres (2½ pints) water

juice of 1 lime

4 tbsp light soy sauce

1 bunch salad onions, thinly sliced

1 tbsp fresh coriander leaves

Step one Remove the skin from the chicken thighs and discard; place the thighs in a large pan. Bruise the lemon grass with a rolling pin and crumple the lime leaves in the palm of your hand. Place in the pan with the garlic, chilli, including the seeds, ginger and water. Bring to the boil and simmer for 30 minutes until the chicken is cooked right through.

Step two Strain the stock into a clean pan then, using 2 forks, shred the meat off the bones. Return the chicken to the pan with the fresh lime juice, soy sauce and sliced salad onions. Heat through gently and, when steaming hot, ladle into bowls. Loosely scatter over the coriander leaves and serve.

This soup is naturally quite low in fat, but for pretty presentation and a little extra flavour, try drizzling a splash of chilli or toasted sesame oil over the surface of each serving.

Chicken Noodle Soup with Lettuce

Noodle soups are the ultimate comfort food. They take very little time to prepare and are also low in fat.

Serves 2

1 tbsp sunflower oil

175g (6oz) boneless, skinless chicken, cut into small pieces

900ml (1½ pints) chicken stock

1 tsp sugar

85g (3¼ oz) packet chicken-flavoured instant noodles

2 salad onions, thinly sliced

50g (2oz) salted peanuts, roughly chopped

50g (2oz) crisp lettuce leaves, shredded

dark soy sauce, to taste

½ x 20g (¾ oz) packet fresh coriander, chopped, to garnish

chilli sauce or chilli oil, to serve

Step one Heat the oil in a large pan. Add the chicken and stir fry for 2–3 minutes until lightly browned and just tender. Pour in the stock and add the sugar, then bring to a gentle simmer and cook for 5 minutes.

Step two While the chicken is simmering, cook the noodles according to the directions on the packet, then drain. Sprinkle half the onions and peanuts into the bottom of 2 large warmed bowls, and add the cooked noodles and lettuce.

Step three Ladle the flavoured stock into the bowls and season with the soy sauce, then scatter over the remaining onions and peanuts. Garnish with the coriander and offer the chilli sauce or oil separately.

Caribbean Cook-up Soup with Dumplings

Anything that's around in the fridge or larder gets thrown into this soup!

Step one Chop each thigh into two or three pieces and cut the steak into chunks. Next, prepare the vegetables: peel and slice the onion, peel and crush the garlic, and peel and roughly dice the yam. De-seed and chop the chilli and, finally, wash and roughly dice the sweet potato. Season the chicken and beef and fry in hot oil for 3–4 minutes until well browned. Add the onion, garlic, yam, chilli, thyme and sweet potato. Stir and cook for another 3–4 minutes.

Step two Add the kidney beans, tomatoes and cinnamon stick, then pour in the beef stock. Bring to the boil, then cover and simmer for approximately 1 hour until the meat is tender.

Step three Meanwhile, make the dumplings. Mix together all the dry ingredients and slowly add enough water to make a soft dough. Using floured hands, shape the dough into balls about the size of whole walnuts, then drop them into the soup. Cover again and cook for 10–15 minutes until the dumplings have puffed up on the surface of the soup. Adjust the seasoning, sprinkle with chopped parsley and serve.

Serves 4

450g (1lb) chicken thighs

450g (1lb) chuck or stewing steak

1 large onion

2 garlic cloves

200g (7oz) yam

1 red chilli

3–4 tbsp vegetable oil

450g (1lb) sweet potatoes

a few sprigs of fresh thyme or ¼ tsp dried thyme

1 x 400g (14oz) tin red kidney beans, drained

1 x 225g (8oz) tin chopped tomatoes

5cm (2in) cinnamon stick

1.75 litres (3 pints) beef stock (use cubes)

salt and freshly ground black pepper

chopped fresh parsley, to garnish

for the dumplings

350g (12oz) plain flour, plus extra for dusting

100g (4oz) cornmeal

¼ tsp dried thyme

½ tsp salt

150–200ml (5–7fl oz) water, to bind

Curried Sweet Potato Soup with Chicken and Spinach

An easy dish for using up leftover roast chicken pieces. If you don't have any, just buy some cooked chicken breasts from the supermarket. Sweet potatoes are a great alternative to normal potatoes, and they add a vibrant colour to this soup.

Serves 4–6

25g (1oz) butter

1 tbsp olive oil

1 onion, chopped

1 leek, chopped

1 celery stick, chopped

2 garlic cloves, crushed

pinch of crushed dried chilli

2 tsp mild curry powder

3 medium-sized sweet potatoes

1.2 litres (2 pints) chicken or vegetable stock

3 cooked chicken breasts, shredded

75g (3oz) young-leaf spinach

salt and freshly ground black pepper

freshly grated nutmeg, to serve

warm garlic naan breads, to serve

Step one Heat the butter and oil in a large saucepan. Add the onion, leek and celery to the pan and cook over a low to medium heat for about 5 minutes until tender but not coloured. Add the garlic, chilli and curry powder and continue to cook for a further minute.

Step two Peel the sweet potatoes and cut into chunks. Add to the pan with the stock, season and bring to the boil. Lower the heat, half-cover the pan and simmer for 20–25 minutes until the potatoes are tender.

Step three Purée the soup until smooth using either a blender or hand-held mixer. Add a little extra stock if the mixture is too thick, and check the seasoning.

Step four Add the chicken to the pan with the spinach. Simmer for a further minute until the chicken has heated through and the spinach has wilted. Ladle into warm bowls and sprinkle a little nutmeg over each bowl. Serve with warm garlic naan breads.

No-need-to-cook Hoisin Spring Rolls

Most of the large supermarkets now stock oriental ingredients, such as rice-paper wrappers. Keep them as a store cupboard ingredient as they are great for a last-minute starter or snack – all you do is soak them in hot water and then fill with your favourite ingredients. Be careful when handling them as they tear quite easily.

Step one Place the rice-paper wrappers in a heatproof bowl and cover with hot water; then leave to soak for 5 minutes until soft and pliable.

Step two In a separate bowl, toss together the carrot, cucumber, salad onions and sesame seeds.

Step three Drain the rice papers on a clean tea towel and spread 1 teaspoon of the hoisin sauce across the centre of each. Sprinkle with a few coriander leaves. Place the vegetables on the rice papers and then the chicken on top. Make sure you don't over-fill the papers as they could split.

Step four Fold two sides in, then roll up to make a neat cylindrical shape. Serve immediately with extra hoisin sauce to dip into.

The spring rolls are not at their best if made up too far ahead of time. Instead, prepare the vegetables and the chicken, cover separately and chill until ready to use.

Serves 4

12 x rice-paper wrappers, each 7.5 x 15cm (3 x 6in)

1 carrot, cut into matchsticks

75g (3oz) piece of cucumber, cut into matchsticks

4 salad onions, shredded

1 tbsp sesame seeds

4 tbsp hoisin sauce, plus extra to serve

small bunch of fresh coriander

350g (12oz) lean cooked chicken, shredded

For more recipes from My Kitchen Table, sign up for our newsletter at www.mykitchentable.co.uk/newsletter

Louisiana Blue Cheese and Chicken Sandwich

Feelin' hot, hot, hot! This tasty chicken sandwich is my best-ever late-night Cajun snack. I raid my fridge and throw in whatever takes my fancy. I usually add a splash of Tabasco sauce for that extra burst of heat. To reduce the fat even further, leave out the blue-cheese mayonnaise.

Serves 1

1 boneless, skinless chicken breast

1 tsp Cajun seasoning or ½ tsp Chinese five-spice powder and a pinch of cayenne pepper

juice of ½ lemon (optional)

15g (½ oz) blue cheese

1 tsp low-fat mayonnaise

4 cherry tomatoes, halved, or 1 small tomato, sliced

1 salad onion, sliced, or a few dice of raw onion

a handful of salad leaves

2 slices bread or 2 large pitta breads, warmed and split open

salt and freshly ground black pepper

Step one Season the chicken with spice, salt and pepper. Cook in a non-stick frying pan for 5 minutes, then turn and cook for about 4 minutes until cooked through but still moist and juicy. Now squeeze over a little lemon juice, if you like.

Step two While the chicken is cooking, mash together the blue cheese and mayonnaise.

Step three Layer the salad ingredients on top of one of the slices of bread or inside the warmed pitta breads and top with moist chicken, followed by the blue-cheese mayo. Sandwich together and eat warm.

Use different types of bread – French bread is equally delicious.

Crunchy Crumbed Chicken Chompers

My kids love chicken chompers, and these taste much nicer than shop-bought nuggets.

Step one Place the breadcrumbs and Parmesan in a shallow dish, season and mix well. Break the eggs into a separate shallow dish and lightly whisk to combine. Put the flour on a flat plate and season generously, stirring to combine.

Step two Cut the chicken fillets into bite-sized chunks, dust in the seasoned flour, tip into the beaten egg and finally roll in the breadcrumb mixture, making sure at each stage that each piece of chicken is well coated. Repeat with the beaten egg-and-breadcrumb mixture until each piece of chicken is double-coated. Arrange on a baking sheet and chill for 10 minutes (or up to 24 hours) to allow the coating to firm up.

Step three Preheat a deep-fat fryer or fill a flat-bottomed wok or frying pan one-third full with sunflower oil and heat to 180°C/350°F. The oil should be hot enough so that when a cube of bread is added to the pan, it browns in about 1 minute.

Step four To make the dips: place half of the mayonnaise in a small bowl, beat in the sweet chilli sauce and season to taste. Put the rest of the mayonnaise into a separate bowl and stir in the mustard and honey. Season to taste.

Step five Deep-fry the chicken chompers in batches for 3–4 minutes until tender and golden brown. Drain on kitchen paper and keep warm until the remainder has been cooked. Pile the chicken chompers onto plates and serve with the dips.

To make your own breadcrumbs lay slices of crustless white bread on a baking sheet in a preheated oven at 110°C/225°F/ gas ¼ and cook for 25–30 minutes until crisp but not coloured. Transfer to a food-processor and blend to fine breadcrumbs. They will keep well in an airtight container for up to 2 weeks.

Serves 4–6

100g (4oz) toasted natural breadcrumbs

50g (2oz) Parmesan, freshly grated

4 eggs

25g (1oz) plain flour

4 boneless, skinless chicken breasts (about 450g/1lb in total)

sunflower oil, for deep-frying

salt and freshly ground black pepper

for the dips

1 x 200g (7oz) jar mayonnaise

2 tbsp sweet chilli sauce

2 tsp wholegrain mustard

½ tsp clear honey

Coconut Chicken Satay Pockets

Chicken fillets (the little pieces underneath regular breasts) are great for this dish because they're exactly the right size. I buy them from my local butcher, but larger supermarkets sell them in packets. If you can only get regular chicken breasts, cut them into 2cm (¾in) wide strips, then bat them out with a rolling pin to flatten them slightly. The result is delicious and exquisite.

Serves 4

1 x 200g (7oz) carton coconut cream

4 tbsp crunchy peanut butter

2 tbsp light soy sauce

1 tbsp runny honey

a few drops of Tabasco sauce

25g (1oz) dry-roasted peanuts, roughly chopped

250g (9oz) chicken fillets

salt and freshly ground black pepper

4 mini naan breads, to serve

1 fresh lime, cut into wedges, to serve

Step one Preheat the grill to high. Soak 4 bamboo skewers in hot water.

Step two Place the coconut cream and peanut butter in a bowl and beat together until well blended. Stir in the light soy sauce, honey, Tabasco and peanuts, and season to taste. If the sauce is too thick, add a little water.

Step three Pour the sauce into a shallow dish and add the chicken fillets, turning to coat them in the sauce. Thread onto the skewers and cook under the grill for 4 minutes on each side until cooked through and well browned.

Step four Warm the naan breads under the grill, then split in half. Remove the chicken fillets from the skewers and push them into the naan breads. Squeeze over a little lime juice and enjoy.

All-American Club Sandwich

There are many types of bread available now. My favourites for sandwiches include malted rye and sourdough breads.

Step one Preheat the grill and cook the bacon until crisp and lightly golden.

Step two Mix the mustard with the mayonnaise and season. Toast the bread and spread with the mustard mayo.

Step three Divide half the lettuce between four slices of the toast, arrange the tomato slices on top and put half the onion slices on top of this. Season to taste. Cover the tomato and onion slices with the chicken, and place a slice of toast on top, mayonnaise-side up.

Step four Add the remaining lettuce followed by the cheese, the bacon and the rest of the onion. Cover with the remaining slices of toast and press down lightly. To serve, cut each sandwich into four triangles and secure each piece with a cocktail stick or small plastic skewer.

Serves 4

12 rindless, smoked streaky bacon rashers

1 tbsp wholegrain mustard

6 tbsp mayonnaise

12 slices white bread

25g (1oz) lettuce, finely shredded

2 tomatoes, sliced

1 onion, thinly sliced

100g (4oz) wafer-thin chicken slices

4 slices Swiss cheese, such as Emmental

salt and freshly ground black pepper

Chicken, Prawn, Mango and Avocado Salad with Ginger-lime Dressing

This delightful salad looks great on the plate and is a joy to eat. Avocado is a fruit rather than a vegetable, and was once called the butter pear because of its creamy consistency. It's used mainly in salads because the flavour is very subtle – some might even say bland. Not me, though – I love it.

Serves 4

2 cooked chicken breasts, skinned and cooled

200g (7oz) cooked, peeled king prawns

1 ripe mango

1 ripe avocado

¼ cucumber, peeled and sliced

4 Little Gem lettuces, leaves separated

100g (4oz) toasted cashews

a handful of fresh small basil leaves

for the dressing

grated zest and juice of 1 lime

2 tsp white wine vinegar

½ tsp grated fresh root ginger

3 tbsp avocado oil or extra-virgin olive oil

salt and freshly ground black pepper

Step one Make the dressing. Place the lime zest in a small bowl, add 1 tablespoon of the lime juice with the vinegar, ginger and oil. Season and mix to combine.

Step two Cut the chicken into bite-sized pieces. Place in a bowl and add the prawns. Peel the mango and cut the 'cheeks' away from the stone. Cut the flesh into chunks and add to the bowl. Cut the avocado in half, discard the stone and skin, then thickly slice the flesh into the bowl. Add the cucumber.

Step three Arrange the lettuce leaves on four plates and top with the chicken mixture. Drizzle over the dressing, then scatter on the cashew nuts and basil. Serve immediately.

Avocado oil is now available in some supermarkets and most health-food shops. For a tropical touch, add some chopped fresh papaya to the salad.

Herby Bulgur Wheat Salad with Chargrilled Chicken and Cucumber-yoghurt Dressing

A colourful and tasty combination. If you have time, make the bulgur salad 2–3 hours in advance to allow the flavours to mingle. If you can't find a fresh pomegranate, use dried cherries instead.

Step one First prepare the dressing. Cut the cucumber in half lengthways and scrape out the seeds using a teaspoon. Coarsely grate half the cucumber, keeping the other half for the salad. Sprinkle with a little salt and place in a sieve over a bowl to drain for 1 hour. Squeeze out any excess moisture from the cucumber, then add the yoghurt and mint. Cover and chill until needed.

Step two Add the bulgur to the boiling water, cover and set aside to soak for about 15 minutes until the grains are tender and have absorbed the water.

Step three Pick out the juicy seeds from the pomegranate, removing all the pith. Finely dice the remaining cucumber. Mix the pomegranate, apricots, pistachios and cucumber into the bulgur. Add the salad onions, herbs and lemon juice and season well.

Step four Preheat a ridged griddle pan. Rub the chicken breasts with the oil and season with salt and cayenne. Cook on the griddle for 4–5 minutes on each side until cooked through. Remove and rest for 5 minutes before slicing each breast on the diagonal into six slices.

Step five Divide the bulgur mixture among four plates, top with some chicken slices and serve with the cucumber yoghurt dressing and warm Mediterranean flatbreads on the side.

Serves 4

100g (4oz) bulgur wheat

300ml (½ pint) boiling water

½ pomegranate

75g (3oz) ready-to-eat dried apricots, roughly chopped

40g (1½ oz) pistachio nuts, roughly chopped

4 salad onions, finely chopped

2 tbsp chopped fresh mint

2 tbsp chopped fresh flat-leaf parsley

juice of 1 lemon

4 skinless chicken breasts

1 tsp olive oil

pinch of cayenne pepper

salt and freshly ground black pepper

warm Mediterranean flatbreads, to serve

for the dressing

½ cucumber

150ml (¼ pint) natural yoghurt

1 tbsp chopped fresh mint

Honeyed Tarragon Quick Chick Salad

I like to cook the chicken on a griddle pan, which gives it lovely markings and a smoky taste, but a frying pan or wok does the job just as well. A bottle or two of iced lager goes down a treat with this salad.

Serves 2

3 tbsp olive oil

grated zest and juice of 1 lemon

1 garlic clove, chopped

1 tbsp chopped fresh tarragon

2 x 100g (4oz) boneless, skinless chicken breasts, each cut into 6–7 slices

1 tsp toasted sesame oil

1–2 tsp clear honey

1 tbsp toasted sesame seeds

3 slices Italian-style bread such as foccacia or ciabatta, toasted and halved

salt and freshly ground black pepper

lettuce leaves and watercress, to serve

Step one Preheat a ridged griddle pan. In a small bowl, mix together 2 tablespoons of the olive oil, the lemon zest, 1 teaspoon of lemon juice, the garlic, tarragon, and salt and pepper. Rub the mixture over the chicken slices, then cook on the griddle, or in a non-stick frying pan or wok, for 4–5 minutes until golden brown.

Step two Meanwhile, make the dressing: mix together the remaining olive oil and lemon juice with the sesame oil, honey and sesame seeds; season with salt and pepper.

Step three Place three pieces of toast on each serving plate and scatter over the lettuce and almost all the watercress. Arrange the chicken slices on top, then spoon over the dressing. Garnish with the remaining watercress and serve.

Chicken and Sun-blushed Tomato Salad

Fragrant chicken and olives, salad leaves and succulent sun-blushed tomatoes make up this tempting salad. To make it more substantial, add steamed baby new potatoes, halved and tossed in a little dressing while they are still warm.

Step one Place the garam masala in a shallow, non-metallic dish with the paprika, cumin, chilli powder, garlic, half the lime juice, ½ a teaspoon each of salt and pepper, and 2 tablespoons of the olive oil. Stir to combine. Cut the chicken breasts into 2cm (¾in) strips and toss in the spice mixture until well coated. Set aside for at least 15 minutes to allow the flavours to develop (or up to 24 hours is fine, covered with clingfilm in the fridge).

Step two Heat a large, non-stick frying pan over a medium heat and add the chicken strips. Cook for about 2 minutes on each side until cooked through and well seared.

Step three Place the remaining lime juice and the honey in a screw-topped jar. Season to taste, then shake vigorously until the salt has dissolved. Add the remaining 4 tablespoons of olive oil and shake again until emulsified.

Step four Tip the salad leaves into a bowl with the sun-blushed tomatoes and olives. Add enough of the dressing to just barely coat the leaves. Divide among serving plates and arrange the seared chicken pieces on top. Serve at once with chunks of ciabatta bread, if liked.

Sun-blushed tomatoes are semi sun-dried and need no soaking. You'll find them in supermarkets on the deli counter, or in the chilled section.

Serves 4

2 tsp garam masala

¼ tsp paprika

¼ tsp ground cumin

1 tsp mild chilli powder

1 garlic clove, crushed

juice of 1 lime

6 tbsp olive oil

4 boneless, skinless chicken breasts (about 450g/1lb in total)

2 tsp clear honey

1 x 200g (7oz) bag Italian-style salad

100g (4oz) sun-blushed tomatoes

100g (4oz) black olives, pitted (good quality, such as Kalamata)

salt and cracked black pepper

ciabatta bread, to serve (optional)

Mediterranean Chicken Caesar with Aïoli and Foccacia Croûtons

This dish takes you on a Mediterranean tour with Italian croûtons, Spanish dressing and Greek-style marinated chicken. Eat it in your back garden on a sunny afternoon and it'll be easy to imagine yourself in a Provençal olive grove.

Serves 4

4 boneless, skinless chicken breasts

1 tbsp chopped fresh rosemary

1 tsp dried oregano

1 shallot, finely chopped

100ml (3½fl oz) red or white wine

2 tbsp olive oil

1 cos lettuce

salt and freshly ground black pepper

for the aïoli

4 tbsp mayonnaise

1 garlic clove, crushed

squeeze of lemon juice

for the croûtons

2 mini foccacia, or half a medium loaf, about 150g (5oz)

1 tbsp olive oil

2 tbsp freshly grated Parmesan

Step one Place the chicken breasts, rosemary, oregano, shallot, wine and olive oil in a shallow dish. Season with salt and pepper and set aside to marinate for at least one hour, but preferably overnight.

Step two Meanwhile, for the aïoli, mix the mayonnaise with the garlic, then squeeze in a little lemon juice to taste.

Step three Preheat the oven to 200°C/400°F/gas 6. Remove the chicken from the marinade and place on a baking sheet. Roast for 15 minutes.

Step four Meanwhile, make the croûtons: cut the foccacia into cubes and toss with the olive oil and Parmesan. Scatter onto a baking sheet, ensuring they are in a single layer. Place in the oven alongside the chicken and bake for 5–10 minutes until both the croûtons and the chicken are crisp and golden brown, and the chicken is cooked through. Remove from the oven and allow the croûtons to cool.

Step five When the chicken has cooled slightly, cut diagonally into strips. Tear the cos lettuce into bite-sized pieces and place in a large salad bowl. Toss with the chicken strips, aïoli and croutons and serve while the chicken is still warm.

Chicken and Pasta Salad with Pine Nuts

This pasta salad is also good served cold, and appeals to children and adults alike.

Step one Preheat the oven to 180°C/350°F/gas 4. Spread out the pine nuts on a baking sheet and toast them in the oven for 8–10 minutes until golden brown. Remove from the oven and leave to cool completely.

Step two Plunge the farfalle into a large pan of boiling, salted water, stir once and cook for 8–10 minutes until al dente or according to the instructions on the packet.

Step three Place the basil in a food-processor with 1 teaspoon of salt and half the garlic, then blend until finely chopped. Add half the pine nuts and all the Parmesan and whizz again briefly. With the machine running, pour in all but 1 tablespoon of the olive oil through the feeder tube until the pesto is thickened and emulsified. Season to taste.

Step four Heat a frying pan until very hot. Place the remaining tablespoon of oil in a bowl with the chicken and the rest of the garlic, season well and mix together. Add the chicken pieces to the pan and cook for 2–3 minutes on each side until cooked through and golden brown. Remove from the heat and fold in the rocket, which will wilt with the heat of the chicken.

Step five When the pasta is cooked, drain, then return to the pan and pour in the pesto, stirring until well coated. Fold in the chicken and rocket mixture with the remaining pine nuts. Season to taste and serve.

Serves 4

100g (4oz) pine nuts

450g (1lb) farfalle pasta

50g (2oz) fresh basil leaves

2 garlic cloves, finely chopped

50g (2oz) Parmesan, freshly grated

150ml (¼ pint) extra-virgin olive oil

2 boneless, skinless chicken breasts, cut widthways into 1cm (½in) strips

50g (2oz) wild rocket

salt and freshly ground black pepper

Southern-style Crunchy Chicken

Well, this is my simple but very tasty version of a famous take-away chicken dish. I actually find it a lot easier to use the oven, as you can cook the whole lot in one go rather than frying it in batches, and once it's in the oven you can leave it alone – until it arrives at the table, that is.

Serves 4

1 medium chicken cut into 8 pieces, or 8 chicken drumsticks and thighs, skin on

1 tbsp vegetable oil

5 tbsp plain flour

1 tbsp Cajun seasoning

1 tsp cayenne pepper

½ tsp salt

Step one Preheat the oven to 220°C/425°F/gas 7. Rub the chicken skin with the oil. Place the flour, Cajun seasoning, cayenne pepper and salt in a large bowl and mix well together.

Step two Toss the chicken pieces in the flour until lightly coated. Place the chicken on a wire rack and sit the rack on a baking sheet. Bake the chicken for 35–45 minutes until cooked through with a good crispy skin. Serve hot and eat with your fingers.

Quick Chicken Liver and Tarragon Pâté

Forget about pâté that takes ages to cook in a water bath. This recipe is incredibly simple and tastes fabulous. Just cook, purée, set and serve. It's as easy as that!

Step one Melt a large knob of the butter in a large frying pan and cook the chicken livers for 3–4 minutes on each side until well browned but still slightly pink in the centre.

Step two Place in a food-processor and whizz until smooth. Add the brandy to the frying pan and swirl round to gather up the pan juices, then add to the food-processor with the garlic, tarragon and the remaining butter. Whizz again until well blended.

Step three Add some salt and pepper followed by the cream and process again until well mixed. Spoon into six ramekins, smoothing the surface level, and leave to cool completely.

Step four To finish off, melt the 50g (2oz) butter and pour over the surface of the pâté. Drop in a few tarragon leaves as garnish. Cover with clingfilm and chill for at least a few hours, or up to 2 days. Serve straight from the fridge with hot, buttered toast, or melba toast if you're feeling posh.

Serves 6

150g (5oz) butter, at room temperature

225g (8oz) chicken livers

2 tbsp brandy

2 garlic cloves, roughly chopped

1 tbsp chopped fresh tarragon

150ml (¼ pint) double cream

salt and freshly ground black pepper

hot, buttered toast, to serve

to garnish

50g (2oz) butter

12 fresh tarragon leaves

Finger-licking Chicken Wings

Chicken wings are inexpensive, cook quickly and make fabulous finger food. Try eating these without licking your fingers!

Serves 4

1 tbsp vegetable oil

1 small onion, very finely chopped

2 garlic cloves, crushed

2 tbsp clear honey

4 tbsp tomato ketchup

4 tbsp Worcestershire sauce

2 tsp English mustard

2 tsp Tabasco sauce

8 chicken wings, tips removed

2 tbsp plain flour, seasoned with salt and freshly ground black pepper

Step one Preheat the oven to 200°C/400°F/gas 6. Heat the oil in a small pan and cook the onion and garlic for 3–4 minutes until softened. Stir in the honey, ketchup, Worcestershire sauce, mustard and Tabasco and simmer very gently for a minute or so.

Step two Dust the chicken in the seasoned flour then brush liberally with the sauce. Place on a baking sheet and roast for 30 minutes until well browned and cooked through.

Step three Transfer to a serving plate and keep those napkins handy, or just lick your fingers!

Light Coronation Chicken

I've slightly updated this classic dish using light yoghurt instead of heavy cream. For convenience, if you're taking it along to a picnic, you can pack it into a cool bag or wide-brimmed vacuum flask. Instead of using breasts you could try roasting a whole chicken and shredding it up. when it's cooled down The leftover carcase can be used to make stock for chicken noodle soup or risotto.

Step one Cut or shred the chicken breast meat into bite-sized pieces and place them in a large bowl. Add the apricots and two-thirds of the almonds.

Step two In another bowl mix together the mayonnaise, yoghurt, mango chutney and curry paste. Season and pour over the chicken. Mix to coat the chicken pieces well in the sauce. Tip into a serving dish, cover and chill for at least 2 hours to allow the flavours to mingle.

Step three Scatter over the remaining almonds and serve with a rice salad.

Serves 4–6

4 cooked chicken breasts, cooled

50g (2oz) ready-to-eat dried apricots, roughly chopped

75g (3oz) toasted flaked almonds

4 rounded tbsp mayonnaise

2 tbsp light Greek yoghurt

2 tbsp mango chutney

1 tbsp medium-hot curry paste

salt and freshly ground black pepper

Tagliatelle with Lemon Chicken, Ricotta and Herbs

If you've got in late and want to knock up something impressive with the least amount of effort, this tasty dish has to be for you. It's one of my midweek saviours. Use ready-cooked chicken breasts for this super-fast supper dish. Egg tagliatelle generally takes less time to cook than other types of pasta, and its lighter texture works well with the ingredients in this recipe. My son likes to mix some crispy bacon pieces into his serving, whilst the missus likes toasted pine nuts, which you might want to try too.

Serves 4

350–400g (12–14oz) tagliatelle

2 cooked chicken breasts

250g (9oz) ricotta

25g (1oz) butter

a handful of wild rocket

2 tbsp roughly chopped fresh flat-leaf parsley

grated zest and juice of 1 lemon

pinch of freshly grated nutmeg

salt and freshly ground black pepper

freshly grated Parmesan, to serve

Step one Bring a large pan of salted water to the boil for the tagliatelle and cook according to the packet instructions.

Step two While the pasta is cooking, cut or shred the chicken breast meat into bite-sized pieces.

Step three Drain the pasta in a colander, reserving a cupful of the cooking water. Tip the pasta back into the pan and add the ricotta, butter, chicken and half the reserved cooking water. Stir to melt the ricotta into the pasta, adding a little more water if it looks dry.

Step four Stir in the rocket, parsley and lemon zest. Season well and add the nutmeg. Add a squeeze of lemon juice and serve immediately with freshly grated Parmesan to hand around.

Strozzapreti with Creamy Pesto Chicken

Pasta is a great standby for those evenings when you have absolutely no time to cook. It's important to remember to stir it once to separate the pasta and to cook at a rolling boil to prevent it from sticking. Strozzapreti is a hand-rolled elongated pasta from Emilia-Romagna, Tuscany and Umbria, and it's available in single and tri-coloured versions. If you cannot find any, substitute another pasta shape.

Step one Bring a large pan of water to a rolling boil and add a good pinch of salt. Add the strozzapreti, stir once and cook for 15 minutes, or according to the packet instructions, until the pasta is al dente.

Step two Meanwhile, heat the olive oil in a heavy-based frying pan. Add the chicken pieces, season generously and sauté for 2–3 minutes until lightly golden on all sides. Stir in the cream and allow to bubble down, then lower the heat and simmer until reduced by one-third. Stir in the pesto and season to taste. The chicken should now be cooked through and tender.

Step three Drain the pasta in a colander and return to the pan. Tip in the chicken and pesto cream, stirring to combine, then fold in two-thirds of the Parmesan. Divide among warmed pasta bowls and scatter the remaining Parmesan on top with a grind or two of pepper to serve.

Serves 4

350g (12oz) strozzapreti

1 tbsp olive oil

225g (8oz) skinless, boneless chicken breasts, cut into bite-sized pieces

300ml (½ pint) double cream

4 tbsp good-quality, ready-made pesto

6 tbsp freshly grated Parmesan

salt and freshly ground black pepper

Spaghetti with Smoked Chicken, Rocket and Cherry Tomatoes

So simple a dish, yet deliciously satisfying.

Serves 4

350g (12oz) spaghetti

4 tbsp extra-virgin olive oil

2 large garlic cloves, finely chopped

275g (10oz) cherry tomatoes, halved

175g (6oz) cooked smoked chicken breast, skinned and cut into strips

75g (3oz) wild rocket

salt and freshly ground black pepper

Step one Bring a large pan of water to a rolling boil and add a good pinch of salt. Swirl in the spaghetti, stir once and cook for 10–12 minutes, or according to the packet instructions, until the pasta is al dente.

Step two Heat half the olive oil in a large frying pan and quickly sauté the garlic for 20–30 seconds until sizzling but not coloured. Tip in the cherry tomatoes, then season generously and continue to sauté for 2–3 minutes until slightly charred but just holding their shape.

Step three Drain the spaghetti and return to the pan, then fold in the cherry tomato mixture with the smoked chicken and rocket until just heated through. Divide among warmed pasta bowls and top with a good grinding of black pepper before serving.

Spiced Chicken, Orange and Watercress Salad

The most intense flavour of an orange comes not from the juice, but from the essential oils in the outer layer of the skin, better known as the zest. When used along with honey and mustard as a marinade for chicken, it helps to make a meal that tastes truly fabulous when cooked.

Step one Toss together the orange zest and juice, honey, wholegrain mustard and chicken strips and leave marinate for at least 30 minutes.

Step two Heat the oil in a wok and stir-fry the chicken strips over a high heat for 4–5 minutes until golden brown and sticky. Add the salad onions, remove from the heat and toss.

Step three Divide the watercress, orange segments and tomatoes between serving plates and spoon the chicken over the top. Drizzle with any pan juices and serve straight away.

Serves 4

finely grated zest and juice of 1 orange

1 tbsp honey

1 heaped tsp wholegrain Dijon mustard

500g (1lb 2oz) skinless, boneless chicken cut into strips

2 tsp sunflower oil

6 salad onions, thinly sliced

120g bag watercress

2 oranges, segmented

100g (4oz) vine-ripened cherry tomatoes, halved

Vietnamese-style Sticky-finger Chicken

Chicken thighs are not only cheaper than breasts, but they can be made much tastier. The secret of this recipe is in the slow cooking, which would leave a chicken breast dry and tasteless. When using thighs you end up with wonderfully succulent, well-flavoured meat. I like to serve these with some steamed fragrant rice and a bowl of stir-fried pak choy.

Serves 4

4 tbsp ketcap manis (Indonesian soy sauce)

1 tbsp grated fresh root ginger

2 garlic cloves, crushed

½ tsp Chinese five-spice powder

8 boneless chicken thighs

1 tbsp sunflower oil

Step one To make the marinade, place the ketcap manis in a bowl with the ginger, garlic and Chinese five-spice, then mix well to combine. Arrange the chicken thighs in a shallow non-metallic dish and pour over the marinade, turning the thighs to coat well. Cover with clingfilm and chill for at least 2 hours (up to 24 hours is best), turning the chicken thighs several times in the marinade. Bring back to room temperature before cooking and wipe off any excess marinade with kitchen paper.

Step two Heat a frying pan over a medium heat. Add the oil to the pan, then place the chicken thighs in it, skin-side down. Reduce the heat to very low and cook for 20–30 minutes until the skin is nice and crispy. Don't be tempted to touch the chicken thighs while they are cooking or shake the pan; just leave them alone and you will produce the most fantastic crispy skin and succulent meat.

Step three When you can see that the chicken thighs are nicely browned and that the flesh is almost but not quite cooked through, turn them over and cook for a further 5–6 minutes until completely cooked through and tender. Remove from the heat and leave to rest in a warm place for 5 minutes. Arrange on warmed plates to serve.

Tender Chicken and Butternut Squash Risotto

When you make this dish any leftovers can go to make delicious risotto cakes. Simply roll and flatten handfuls of cold risotto into patties, coat in a mixture of breadcrumbs and Parmesan, and fry them in butter.

Step one Preheat the oven to 200°C/400°F/gas 6. Arrange the chicken thighs in a small roasting tin and season. Roast for about 40 minutes until cooked through and tender. Remove from the oven and leave to cool, then cut the chicken into bite-sized pieces, discarding the skin and bones. Set aside on a plate.

Step two Heat half of the oil in a large sauté pan, add the butternut squash and season. Cook over a fairly high heat for about 5 minutes, tossing occasionally, until lightly caramelised. Reduce the heat, add half of the leeks and cook over a gentle heat for a further 2–3 minutes, stirring occasionally, until the butternut squash is completely tender when pierced with the tip of a sharp knife. Tip into a bowl and set aside until ready to use.

Step three Pour the stock into a large pan and bring to a gentle simmer. Wipe out the pan used to cook the squash and return it to the heat. Add the remaining oil, then cook the rest of the leeks for a few minutes, stirring, until softened but not coloured.

Step four Add the rice to the leek mixture and continue to cook for another minute, stirring to ensure that all the grains are well coated. Add a ladleful of the simmering stock to the pan, stirring continuously until all the liquid has been absorbed. Continue adding ladlefuls of the stock, stirring all the time and making sure that each ladleful is absorbed before adding the next. The whole process takes about 18–20 minutes.

Step five Add the reserved chicken and the butternut squash mixture to the risotto pan and give it a quick vigorous mix to combine and heat through. Season to taste and serve.

Serves 4–6

4 whole chicken thighs

4 tbsp olive oil

1 butternut squash, peeled, seeded and diced

2 large leeks, trimmed and finely chopped

1.2 litres (2 pints) chicken stock

350g (12oz) risotto rice (Carnaroli or Arborio)

sea salt and freshly ground black pepper

Oriental Steamed Soy Chicken and Vegetables

For a really delicious low-fat meal that's healthy and so easy, make a date with my Oriental Steamed Soy Chicken – you'll be hooked. To make this recipe you will need a large, two-tiered oriental bamboo steamer.

Serves 2

4 tbsp soy sauce

1 tbsp honey

pinch of crushed dried chilli

2 chicken breasts or 4 chicken thighs, skinned, boned and cut into strips

100g (4oz) choy sum or pak choy

75g (3oz) shiitake mushrooms

50g (2oz) beansprouts

2 salad onions, thinly sliced

boiled rice, to serve

Step one In a shallow bowl, mix together the soy sauce, honey and chilli. Add the chicken pieces, then place the bowl in a bamboo steamer. Cover and set over a pan of boiling water to cook for 10 minutes.

Step two Cut the choy sum into 12cm (4¾in) lengths, or quarter the pak choy, and halve the mushrooms. Toss together and place in a second layer of the bamboo steamer. Scatter the beansprouts and salad onions over the top.

Step three Lift the steamer containing the chicken off the top of the pan and sit the vegetable tier underneath – it is crucial that the vegetables sit beneath the chicken otherwise the juices they release will all fall into the bowl holding the chicken and dilute the soy dressing.

Step four Return the bamboo stack to the pan and continue to steam for a further 3–4 minutes until the vegetables are tender but still crisp and the chicken is cooked through.

Step five Serve the bamboo steamer stack at the table with the rice, and allow guests to help themselves.

Soy-poached Chicken Breasts with Pak Choy, Coconut Rice and Hot and Sour Sauce

People sometimes say they prefer a nice juicy thigh or leg of chicken because they find the breast too dry. That's often because it's been overcooked. Poaching helps to avoid this, and it's also a healthy way of cooking, but don't overdo it: the chicken should be lovely and moist, not falling to bits. If you're short of time, you can use a ready-made oyster sauce instead of making the hot and sour sauce.

Step one Place the rice in a bowl, cover with cold water and soak for 15–20 minutes, then drain and rinse. Tip into a saucepan and add the coconut milk, 300ml (½ pint) water and a pinch of salt. Bring to the boil and reduce the heat to a very gentle simmer. Cover and cook for 10 minutes until the rice is tender.

Step two While the rice is cooking, shred the lime leaves and place them in a saucepan. Peel and slice the ginger and garlic and roughly chop the chilli, then add to the pan with the soy sauce and 600ml (1 pint) water. Bring to the boil, then add the chicken breasts, cover and cook over a low heat for 4 minutes. Turn the chicken in the liquid and simmer for a further 2 minutes until cooked through.

Step three Meanwhile, trim the pak choy, cut them in half through the root and cook in a steamer set over the chicken pan for 3 minutes until tender.

Step four Make the sauce while the pak choy is steaming. Whisk all the ingredients together in a small saucepan, place over a medium heat and bring to the boil. Simmer for 1 minute, stirring constantly, until thickened and glossy.

Step five Slice the chicken and arrange on plates or in bowls with the coconut rice and pak choy. Drizzle over the sauce, scatter on the salad onions and sesame seeds, and serve.

Serves 4

225g (8oz) basmati rice

150ml (¼ pint) coconut milk

2 kaffir lime leaves

2cm (¾in) piece of fresh root ginger

1 garlic clove

½ large red chilli, seeded

1 tbsp light soy sauce

4 skinless chicken breasts

4 heads pak choy

salt

4 salad onions, chopped, to serve

1 tbsp toasted sesame seeds, to serve

for the sauce

4 tbsp caster sugar

1 heaped tsp cornflour

4 tbsp rice vinegar

4 tbsp light soy sauce

2 tbsp rice wine or dry sherry

Crispy Chicken Thighs with Savoury Puy Lentil Ragout

If you can't find Puy, I've used green or brown lentils with much success.

Serves 4

8 whole chicken thighs

2 leeks, trimmed and finely diced

2 carrots, finely diced

2 celery sticks, finely diced

3 tbsp olive oil

225g (8oz) dried Puy lentils

sea salt and freshly ground black pepper

Step one Remove the bones from the chicken thighs and trim down the thigh meat. Place the bones and trimmings in a pan with half of the leeks, carrots and celery. Pour in 1.2 litres (2 pints) of water and bring to the boil, then reduce the heat and simmer for about 1 hour. Strain the stock through a fine sieve and place in a jug. You will need about 300ml (½ pint) in total so you can reduce it down further after straining if you need to.

Step two Heat a frying pan over a medium heat. Add 1 tablespoon of the oil to the pan and place the chicken thighs in, skin-side down. Reduce the heat to very low and cook for 20–25 minutes until the skin is nice and crispy. Don't touch the chicken thighs while they are cooking.

Step three When you can see that the chicken thighs are nicely browned, turn them over and cook for a further 5–6 minutes until completely cooked and tender. Remove from the heat and leave to rest in a warm place for 5 minutes.

Step four While the chicken thighs are cooking, rinse the lentils in a sieve under cold running water, then place in a pan with 600ml (1 pint) of water. Add a pinch of salt and bring to the boil, then reduce the heat and simmer for 15–20 minutes until al dente. Drain in a sieve and set aside.

Step five Meanwhile, heat the remaining oil in a pan and gently cook the rest of the leeks, carrots and celery for about 10 minutes until softened but not coloured. Stir in the cooked lentils and the stock. Season to taste and simmer for a few minutes until most of the stock has been absorbed and the vegetables are lovely and tender. Carve each chicken thigh into two or three slices. Spoon the savoury lentils onto warmed plates and arrange the slices of crispy chicken on top to serve.

Zesty Chick Fric

This is just like that old classic, fricassee, and by having the chicken boned you'll save bags of time. Using thighs keeps the meat juicy, just the way I like it. You can use the egg whites to make a quick dessert.

Step one Heat a heavy-based frying pan. Cut each chicken thigh into four pieces and place skin-side down in the frying pan. Cook for 8–10 minutes, turning once, until crisp and golden brown. Cook the rice according to the packet instructions.

Step two Heat the olive oil in a large sauté pan or a frying pan with a lid and cook the onion, carrot, celery and garlic for 3–4 minutes, stirring, until golden. Add the flour to the vegetables, stirring with a wooden spoon, and cook for 1 minute before gradually adding the stock and lemon zest. Bring to the boil, then simmer for 3–4 minutes.

Step three Add the chicken to the pan of saucy vegetables, cover and simmer for 3 minutes until the vegetables are tender.

Step four Stir the peas and plenty of salt and pepper into the chicken mixture and cook for 1–2 minutes. Beat the egg yolks, then stir in the lemon juice. Over a gentle heat, add the egg yolk mixture to the chicken and stir for a few minutes to thicken the sauce, then stir in the parsley. Season to taste.

Step five Spoon the chicken mixture onto a serving plate, garnish with lemon slices, and serve with the rice.

Serves 2

4 boneless chicken thighs

1 x 120g (4⅓ oz) pack boil-in-the-bag basmati rice

2 tbsp olive oil

1 large onion, thinly sliced

1 carrot, diced

1 celery stick, roughly diced

1 garlic clove, finely chopped

1 tbsp plain flour

300ml (½ pint) hot chicken stock

grated zest and juice of 1 lemon

50g (2oz) frozen peas

3 egg yolks

2 tbsp chopped fresh parsley

salt and freshly ground black pepper

quartered lemon slices, to garnish

Chicken Livers and Bacon with Tsar Mash

Some things we like, some things we're not too sure about. Well, if you like chicken livers this recipe will be used again and again; if you're not sure, it's bound to win you over. It has a real explosive taste that leaves the dishes satisfyingly clean. Buy the chicken livers from your butcher, or check out the freezer section in your supermarket.

Serves 2

500g (1lb 2oz) floury potatoes, peeled and diced

1 tbsp olive oil

4 rashers streaky bacon

200g (7oz) trimmed chicken livers

1 tbsp red wine vinegar

2 tbsp port

1 x 150g (5oz) carton soured cream

salt and freshly ground black pepper

snipped chives, to garnish

Step one Cook the potatoes in a large pan of boiling, salted water for 8–10 minutes until tender.

Step two Heat the oil in a large frying pan and cook the bacon for 1 minute. Add the chicken livers to the pan and cook over a high heat for 1–2 minutes on each side until well browned but still pink in the centre; season to taste. Transfer to a heatproof dish and place in the bottom of the heated oven to keep warm.

Step three Pour the vinegar and port into the hot pan and bubble vigorously for 1 minute. Stir in half the soured cream, lower the heat and simmer gently for 2–3 minutes until thickened.

Step four Drain the potatoes and return them to the pan. Mash well, then beat in the remaining soured cream; season to taste.

Step five Pile the mash onto two serving plates and spoon the liver and bacon on top. Season the soured cream sauce and drizzle over. Garnish with snipped chives and coarsely ground black pepper and serve immediately.

Cha-cha-cha Chimichangas

Chimichangas are simply fried Mexican tortillas. They'll get you cha-cha-cha-ing around your kitchen.

Step one Heat the sunflower oil in a large pan and stir-fry the onion, pepper and chicken thighs over a high heat for 3–4 minutes until well browned. Stir in the chillies, garlic, tomatoes and sweetcorn and cook for a further 2–3 minutes until the chicken is cooked through. Stir in the taco sauce and salad onions and set aside to cool a little.

Step two Warm one of the tortillas in a hot, dry frying pan until soft and flexible. Spoon a quarter of the cooled chicken mixture into the centre of the tortilla and fold over the edges to form a neat parcel; pin in place with wooden cocktail sticks. Repeat with the remaining tortillas.

Step three Heat 1cm (½in) vegetable oil in a large frying pan and cook the chimichangas for 2–3 minutes on each side until crisp and golden brown. Drain on kitchen paper and serve hot with shredded lettuce, soured cream and guacamole.

Serves 4

sunflower oil, for frying

1 onion, finely chopped

1 red pepper, seeded and diced

2 boneless, skinless chicken thighs, roughly chopped

2 green chillies, seeded and thinly sliced

2 garlic cloves, finely chopped

2 tomatoes, roughly chopped

100g (4oz) frozen sweetcorn, thawed

4 tbsp taco sauce

4 salad onions, finely chopped

4 large flour tortillas

shredded lettuce, soured cream and ready-made guacamole, to serve

Doodle Spinach 'n' Chicken Noodle

This succulent and nutritious dish, with a hint of the Orient, cooks in a flash and tastes divine. If you've got greens instead of spinach, that'll do fine too.

Serves 2

175g (6oz) egg noodles

1 tbsp sunflower oil

2 small boneless, skinless chicken breasts, thinly sliced diagonally

1 bunch salad onions, trimmed and halved widthways

1 garlic clove, sliced

100g (4oz) chestnut mushrooms, sliced

1½ tsp coarsely crushed black peppercorns

3 tbsp oyster sauce

100ml (3½ fl oz) chicken stock

100g (4oz) spinach leaves, cut into large strips (remove any tough stalks)

salt and freshly ground black pepper

Step one Cook the noodles in boiling water for about 4 minutes, or according to the packet instructions. Drain well, set aside and keep warm.

Step two Meanwhile, heat the sunflower oil in a frying pan, then add the chicken slices, season and cook over a high heat for 3–4 minutes until browned and almost cooked through. Add the salad onions, garlic, mushrooms and crushed peppercorns to the pan and cook, stirring, for 2 minutes.

Step three Add the oyster sauce and stock to the pan, stirring to heat through. Add the spinach and cook for 1–2 minutes until just wilted. Stir and season with salt, then serve on a bed of noodles.

Wok-it Chicken Chow Mein

For this quick noodle dish, shredded cooked chicken is stir-fried with garlic, ginger, soy sauce and chilli sauce and tossed through crunchy vegetables and tasty noodles – perfect for a quick supper.

Step one Cook the noodles in a large pan of boiling, salted water according to the packet instructions.

Step two Meanwhile, heat the oil in a wok or large frying pan and stir-fry the onion over a high heat for 2–3 minutes until beginning to brown. Add the garlic, ginger (if using), beansprouts and mangetout or peas and stir-fry for 1 minute.

Step three Drain the noodles well and add to the wok or frying pan with the chicken and soy sauce; cook for 2 minutes until piping hot. Stir in the sweet chilli sauce and serve immediately.

Try making this with different kinds of noodles, such as udon or rice noodles.

Serves 3

175g (6oz) noodles

2 tsp sunflower oil

1 onion, thinly sliced

2 garlic cloves, thinly sliced

1cm (½in) piece of fresh root ginger, finely chopped (optional)

175g (6oz) beansprouts

175g (6oz) mangetout, halved lengthways, or peas, thawed if frozen

225g (8oz) lean cooked chicken, shredded

2 tbsp soy sauce

2 tbsp sweet chilli sauce

For a video masterclass on knife skills, go to
www.mykitchentable.co.uk/videos/knifeskills

75

Charred Chicken and Pepper Fajitas

The sight and sound of sizzling chicken and vegetables arriving at your table is a joy, and it doesn't have to be limited to a restaurant; this dish can be made at home with surprisingly little effort. It's so simple that once you've tried it it's sure to be a favourite.

Serves 2

2 large boneless, skinless chicken breasts, cut into 1cm (½ in) wide strips

1 yellow pepper, seeded and cut lengthways into 1cm (½ in) wide strips

1 red pepper, seeded and cut lengthways into 1cm (½ in) wide strips

1 red onion, thickly sliced

½ tsp dried oregano

¼ tsp crushed dried chilli

1 tbsp vegetable oil

grated zest and juice of 1 lime, plus an extra lime for serving

4 x 20cm (8in) flour tortillas

leafy salad

150ml (¼ pint) 0% fat Greek yoghurt

salt and freshly ground black pepper

coriander to garnish (optional)

Step one Place the chicken strips, peppers, onion, oregano, chilli, vegetable oil, and lime zest and juice in a large bowl. Add plenty of seasoning and toss together until well mixed.

Step two Heat a flat griddle pan or heavy, non-stick frying pan. Add the chicken mixture and cook over a high heat for 6–8 minutes, turning once or twice, until the mixture is well browned, lightly charred and cooked through.

Step three Warm the tortillas in the microwave or in a dry frying pan for a few seconds.

Step four Serve separately, or pile the chicken mixture in the middle of your warm tortillas, add salad, a squeeze of the extra lime, a sprinkle of coriander leaves and a dollop of yoghurt, then roll up and enjoy.

Pan-fried Chicken with Corncakes

Corn- or maize-fed chickens have a distinctive colour, and marinating their meat in buttermilk helps retain their delicious moistness. I've used the rest of the buttermilk to make corncakes.

Step one Place the buttermilk in a bowl with the garlic, season and add the chicken, turning to coat. Set aside for 5 minutes.

Step two In a bowl or plastic bag, combine the cayenne pepper with 4 tablespoons of the flour and 1 teaspoon each of salt and pepper. One by one, lift the chicken breasts out of the buttermilk, shaking off any excess, and dip into the flour mixture to coat evenly, again shaking off any excess. Reserve the remaining buttermilk mixture.

Step three Heat a 0.5cm (¼in) layer of oil in a large frying pan. Add the chicken, skin-side down, and cook for 8 minutes until the skin is crisp and browned. Turn the chicken over and cook for a further 2–3 minutes until golden. Drain on kitchen paper and transfer to a warm plate. Keep hot.

Step four Sift the remaining flour and the cornflour into a bowl and add ½ a teaspoon of salt and 1 teaspoon of pepper. Make a well in the centre and pour in the eggs and 6 tablespoons of the reserved buttermilk mixture. Beat until smooth. Stir in the salad onions, parsley and sweetcorn.

Step five Place a large, non-stick frying pan over a medium heat, add 2 tablespoons of oil and swirl around until heated, then spoon in ladlefuls of the batter – you'll need eight corncakes in total so, depending on the size of your pan, you may need to make them in batches. Cook for 3–4 minutes on each side until crisp and lightly golden. Drain on kitchen paper.

Step six Place two corncakes on each warmed serving plate. Place the rested chicken on top. Serve with a separate bowl of ranchero or barbecue sauce.

Serves 4

120ml (4fl oz) cultured buttermilk

2 garlic cloves, crushed

4 x 75g (3oz) boneless chicken breasts (corn-fed, if possible)

1 tsp cayenne pepper

100g (4oz) self-raising flour

sunflower oil, for frying

50g (2oz) cornflour

2 eggs, beaten

4 salad onions, finely chopped

1 tbsp chopped fresh flat-leaf parsley, plus extra to garnish

1 x 325g (10½ oz) tin sweetcorn kernels, drained and rinsed

salt and freshly ground black pepper

shop-bought ranchero or chunky barbecue sauce, to serve

Crispy Lemon Fusion Chicken

This may seem rather strange at first, cooking the floured chicken without any added fat, but providing you cook it good and slow, the skin will gradually release enough fat to prevent any burning. The wine and stock are nicely thickened up by the cornflour, making a delicious France-meets-China fusion dish that you could serve French-style with puréed potatoes and green beans, or Chinese-style with boiled rice, pak choy and a splash of soy sauce.

Serves 4

2 garlic cloves, finely chopped

grated zest and juice of 1 lemon

2 tsp Dijon mustard

1 tsp fresh thyme leaves, plus 4 sprigs

8 boneless chicken thighs, skin on

3 tbsp cornflour

100ml (3½ fl oz) white wine

100ml (3½ fl oz) chicken stock

salt and freshly ground black pepper

Step one Mix together the garlic, lemon zest, mustard, thyme leaves and some salt and pepper. Season the chicken thighs, then pull the skin back from the flesh. Spread with the mustard mixture, then stretch the skin back into place.

Step two Season the cornflour with salt and pepper, then roll the chicken thighs in the mixture. Set a large non-stick frying pan over a low heat and, when hot, add the chicken thighs, skin-side down. Cook for 20 minutes without turning until the skin is crunchy and deep golden and the chicken is almost completely cooked through.

Step three Turn over the chicken and pour off any excess fat. Pour in the wine and lemon juice and add the thyme sprigs, then raise the heat and bubble rapidly for 3–4 minutes. Add the stock and simmer for a further 2–3 minutes until the sauce is smooth and thickened and the chicken is cooked through. Serve warm.

Hoisin and Honey Chicken Stir-fry

The secret of a good stir-fry is to have everything prepared in advance, cut roughly into the same size and ready to go into your hot wok at a moment's notice. Remember to keep it hot, hot, hot for that authentic taste.

Step one Chop the celery, carrot, peppers, broccoli, corn cobs and mushrooms wither horizontally into slices, or lengthways into batons.

Step two Mix the chicken with the soy sauce and toasted sesame oil. Heat a wok or large frying pan and pour in the groundnut oil. Swirl the oil around the wok so that it's well coated, then add the chicken and stir-fry for 2–3 minutes. Remove with a slotted spoon and keep warm.

Step three Throw the salad onions, garlic and ginger into the wok and fry for 30 seconds, then add all the prepared vegetables except the beansprouts, and continue to stir-fry over a high heat for 2–3 minutes until crisp and tender. Now add the beansprouts, chicken, honey, hoisin sauce and water. Toss and heat for 3–4 minutes. Season with pepper and serve with steamed rice or noodles.

Serves 4

1 celery stick

1 carrot, peeled

½ red pepper, seeded

½ green pepper, seeded

1 small head broccoli

4 baby corn cobs

6 button mushrooms

2 plump, boneless chicken breasts, cut into strips 1cm (½ in) wide and 7.5cm (3in) long

2 tbsp soy sauce

1 tbsp toasted sesame oil

2 tbsp groundnut oil

3 salad onions, sliced at an angle

1 garlic clove, chopped

2.5cm (1in) piece of fresh root ginger, finely chopped

75g (3oz) beansprouts

2 tbsp clear honey

2 tbsp hoisin sauce

2 tbsp water

freshly ground black pepper

steamed rice or noodles, to serve

Scrunchy Sweet and Sour Chicken

Chicken and pineapple is a wonderful combination, and this dish shows it off to great effect. It has a lovely fresh flavour that's sure to be popular with all the family. I like to serve it with egg-fried rice.

Serves 4

2 egg yolks

2 tbsp cornflour

vegetable oil, for deep-frying

4 boneless, skinless chicken breasts, cubed

salt and freshly ground black pepper

for the sweet and sour sauce

1 onion, sliced

1 small red pepper, seeded and cut into 2.5cm (1in) pieces

1 small orange pepper, seeded and cut into 2.5cm (1in) pieces

1 x 435g (15oz) tin pineapple cubes in natural juice

1 tbsp cornflour

2 tbsp tomato ketchup

2 tbsp light soy sauce

1 tbsp white wine vinegar

handful of fresh coriander leaves, to garnish

Step one Mix together the egg yolks with 1 tablespoon of water, the cornflour and some salt and pepper.

Step two Heat 5cm (2in) of oil in a wok or deep frying pan. Toss the chicken in the cornflour mixture and deep-fry in batches for 5 minutes or so until crisp and golden. Drain on kitchen paper.

Step three Empty the oil from the wok to leave a thin coating in the pan. Stir-fry the onion and peppers over a high heat for 2–3 minutes. Drain the pineapple cubes (reserving the juice), add to the pan and cook for a minute or two.

Step four Mix together the cornflour and a little of the pineapple juice to form a paste, then stir in the remaining juice, the ketchup, soy sauce, vinegar and 135ml (4½fl oz) water. Pour this into the pan and bring to the boil, stirring until the mixture thickens.

Step five Stir the chicken pieces into the pan and simmer for 5 minutes until cooked through. Check the seasoning, then divide among bowls, scatter over the coriander and serve.

Sauté of Chicken with Tarragon Cream Sauce

Any combination of potato and vegetable will complement this simple yet sophisticated dish.

Step one Heat the butter and oil in a sauté pan. Season the chicken breasts on both sides and cook for 1–2 minutes on each side until browned. Add the wine and allow to bubble, then reduce for 3–4 minutes over a high heat, turning the breasts occasionally.

Step two Add the cream and tarragon to the pan and season generously. Cook gently for another 3–4 minutes, basting the chicken breasts with the sauce occasionally, until they are cooked through. Arrange the chicken on warmed plates and spoon over the sauce to serve.

Serves 4

50g (2oz) butter

1 tbsp olive oil

4 x 100g (4oz) skinless chicken breasts

120ml (4fl oz) dry white wine

150ml (¼ pint) double cream

2 tbsp chopped fresh tarragon

sea salt and freshly ground black pepper

Chicken Kiev with Cheese and Butterbean Mash

Chicken Kiev is one of those old favourites that everyone loves.

Serves 2

2 x 75g (3oz) boneless, skinless chicken breasts

40g (1½ oz) unsalted butter, at room temperature

4 tbsp chopped fresh parsley

2 garlic cloves, crushed

50g (2oz) fresh white breadcrumbs

1 tbsp freshly grated Parmesan

1 tbsp seasoned plain flour

1 egg, beaten

1–2 tbsp vegetable oil

for the purée

1 tbsp olive oil

1 small onion, finely chopped

1 x 400g (14oz) tin butter beans, drained

75g (3oz) mature Cheddar or Gruyère, finely diced

knob of butter

2 tbsp chopped fresh coriander (optional)

a few drops of Tabasco sauce

salt and freshly ground black pepper

Step one Using a small knife, horizontally cut a pocket into each chicken breast. Mix together the butter, parsley, garlic and plenty of salt and pepper. Divide the mixture between the chicken breast pockets.

Step two Stir together the breadcrumbs and Parmesan cheese. Dust the chicken breasts in the seasoned flour, then coat them in the beaten egg and, finally, roll them in the breadcrumb mixture. Heat the vegetable oil in a large frying pan and cook the chicken for 5–6 minutes on each side until golden brown and cooked through.

Step three To make the butter bean purée, heat the olive oil in a small pan and cook the onion for 5 minutes until softened. Add the beans to the pan and cook gently for 2–3 minutes, stirring occasionally, until warmed through. Add the cheese to the pan with the butter, stirring until melted. Using a hand blender, whizz the mixture until smooth and creamy. Stir in the coriander, if using, and add salt, pepper and Tabasco to taste.

Step four Spoon the purée onto serving plates and top with the chicken Kiev. Serve straight away.

Ginger Chicken with Coconut Rice

The delicious smells coming from the oven once this is on the go will drive your family's tastebuds wild.

Step one Preheat the oven to 190°C/375°F/gas 5. Heat the oil in a frying pan and cook the chicken, skin-side down, for 2–3 minutes on each side until golden brown; transfer to an ovenproof dish.

Step two Mix together the honey, soy sauce, garlic, ginger and zest and juice of the orange, and pour the mixture over the chicken. Bake for 10 minutes, then add the mushrooms and salad onions. Baste the chicken with the juices and bake for a further 10 minutes.

Step three Meanwhile, make the coconut rice: bring the water to the boil in a non-stick pan, add the creamed coconut and stir until it has dissolved; add the rice and bay leaf. Cover and simmer for 12–15 minutes, stirring occasionally, until the rice is tender and the liquid absorbed.

Step four Serve the rice with the chicken, garnished with orange wedges and bay leaves.

Serves 4

1 tbsp vegetable oil

4 boneless chicken breasts, skin on

2 tbsp clear honey

1 tbsp dark soy sauce

2 garlic cloves, crushed

2cm (¾in) piece of fresh root ginger, finely grated

grated zest and juice of 1 large orange

225g (8oz) button mushrooms, halved lengthways

2 bunches salad onions, trimmed and halved

400ml (14fl oz) of water

1 x 50g (2oz) block creamed coconut, roughly chopped

200g (7oz) long grain rice

1 bay leaf

orange wedges and bay leaves, to garnish

Cajun Chicken Fillets with Spanish Orange Salad

These Cajun-spiced chicken fillets are served on top of a juicy, leafy salad – it's a sizzling combination! Look out for mini chicken fillets in your local supermarket; they are ideal for this quick tasty recipe, but if you can't get hold of them use standard chicken breasts, thinly sliced.

Serves 4

for the Cajun chicken

12 mini skinless chicken breast fillets

juice of 1 lime

5 tbsp plain flour

1 tbsp Cajun seasoning

1 tsp cayenne pepper

½ tsp salt

for the salad

2 oranges

1 x 120g (4½ oz) bag spinach and rocket salad

1 tbsp olive oil

1 small red onion, thinly sliced

Step one Preheat the oven to 220°C/425°F/gas 7. Toss the chicken in the lime juice to coat. Place the flour, Cajun seasoning, cayenne pepper and salt into a large bowl and mix well together.

Step two Sprinkle the flour mixture onto a plate. Lift the chicken pieces out of the lime juice and press each side into the seasoned flour to coat evenly. Place the chicken on a wire rack and sit the rack on a baking sheet. Bake for 15–20 minutes.

Step three While the chicken is cooking peel the oranges, discarding the white pith. Cut into segments over a bowl to catch all the juice – this will make the basis of your dressing.

Step four Toss the orange segments with the orange juice, salad leaves, oil and onion and divide among individual serving plates. Pile the crispy Cajun chicken on top to serve.

Roast Honey Lemon and Garlic Herb Chicken

Lemon chicken is one of my favourite dishes – the acidity from the lemons makes a wonderful marinade and helps make the chicken beautifully tender. I sometimes roast some extra lemon wedges in with the chicken and serve them as a garnish.

Step one Season the chicken. Mix together the garlic, lemon zest and juice, chilli, honey and ground coriander in a non-metallic dish. Turn the chicken in the marinade to coat, then cover and marinate in the fridge for 2–3 hours or overnight.

Step two Preheat the oven to 200°C/400°F/gas 6. Roast the chicken in the marinade for 25–30 minutes until the chicken is tender.

Step three Place the chicken breasts on warmed serving plates and garnish with sprigs of fresh coriander and roast lemon wedges. Serve with roasted vine tomatoes, if liked.

Serves 4

4 boneless, skinless chicken breasts

3 garlic cloves, crushed

finely grated zest and juice of 3 lemons

1 red chilli, seeded and finely chopped

4 tbsp clear honey

2 tbsp ground coriander

salt and freshly ground black pepper

small handful of fresh coriander, roasted lemon wedges and vine tomatoes, to serve

For a video masterclass on marinating meat, go to
www.mykitchentable.co.uk/videos/marinatingmeat

KITCHEN TABLE

Roasted Chicken Breast with Courgette Stuffing

If you fancy a spot of gravy with this dish, simply stir a tablespoon of plain flour into the cooking juices, then gradually whisk in 120ml (4fl oz) of chicken stock. Simmer for a couple of minutes, sieve and serve.

Serves 4

2 courgettes (about 225g/8oz in total)

40g (1½oz) unsalted butter, at room temperature

1 small onion, finely chopped

50g (2oz) full-fat cream cheese

25g (1oz) fine white breadcrumbs, made from day-old bread

1 egg yolk

2 tbsp chopped fresh mixed herbs (such as tarragon, parsley and chervil)

2 tbsp freshly grated Parmesan

4 large boneless chicken breasts, skin on

1 tbsp olive oil

salt and freshly ground black pepper

roasted new potatoes, to serve

Step one Preheat the oven to 200°C/400°F/gas 6. Top and tail the courgettes, then coarsely grate in a food-processor, or use a mandolin or box grater. Tip into a clean tea towel and squeeze out any excess moisture.

Step two Melt a knob of the butter in a large, ovenproof frying pan. Add the onion and cook for 2–3 minutes until softened but not browned. Add the grated courgettes, increase the heat and sauté for 3–4 minutes. Tip onto a plate to cool a little.

Step three Using a fork, soften the remaining butter in a bowl, then beat in the cream cheese. Mix in half the breadcrumbs, the egg yolk, herbs, and onion and courgette mixture, mixing well. Stir in the remaining breadcrumbs and Parmesan, and season.

Step four Using a sharp knife, make a pocket in each chicken breast by cutting horizontally almost all the way through but leaving them attached at one side, then push about a tablespoon of the stuffing into each, spreading it with a round-bladed knife. Carefully lift the skin of each breast and spread a little more of the stuffing between the flesh and the skin, then seal and secure with wooden cocktail sticks. Season all over.

Step five Wipe out the frying pan and return to the heat. Add the olive oil, then cook the chicken breasts skin-side down for 3–4 minutes until golden, turning once. Transfer to the oven and cook for a further 15–20 minutes or until cooked through. Remove from the oven and leave to rest for 5 minutes. Carve each chicken breast into three slices and arrange on warmed serving plates with roasted new potatoes.

Chicken, Sage and Cheddar En Croûte

Delicious straight from the oven or cooled and packed into a lunch box or picnic basket to serve with a simple green salad.

Step one Preheat the oven to 200°C/400°F/gas 6. Open out the pastry on a lightly floured board and roll out slightly so it is large enough to cut into four 15 x 20cm (6 x 8in) rectangles. Spread mustard over the centre of each rectangle and place a chicken breast on each. Season with salt and pepper, then place 2 sage leaves on each fillet.

Step two Scatter the cheese evenly over the chicken, then dampen the edges of the pastry with a little water. Fold the pastry over to enclose the filling, squeezing together the edges between finger and thumb to ensure no melted cheese can escape during baking.

Step three Transfer the parcels to a baking sheet, seam-side down, then brush each with a little milk. Bake for 25 minutes until the pastry is crisp and deep golden and the chicken is cooked through. Serve hot or cold.

If you want to decorate your parcels, use a small, sharp knife to score a sage-shaped leaf on top of each before brushing with milk and baking. Alternatively, if you have any pastry trimmings left over, re-roll them, cut out leaf shapes and stick one to the surface of each parcel with a little water before baking.

Serves 4

1 x 375g (13oz) pack ready-rolled puff pastry

4 small boneless, skinless chicken breasts, each about 75g (3oz)

1 tbsp Dijon mustard

8 fresh sage leaves

150g (5oz) Cheddar, coarsely grated

1 tbsp milk

salt and freshly ground black pepper

Superb Lemon-herb Chicken with Roast Potatoes

I know everyone thinks they know how to roast a chicken, but as this is the best recipe for a roast chicken in the whole world, I thought I'd share it with you. I have a chicken brick that I often cook this in, as it comes out moist and juicy with a miraculously crisp skin. If you don't own one (they cost around £10 from cook shops), roast the chicken in the oven as detailed here. And don't save roast chicken and potatoes for Sundays – it's ideal for a casual after-work dinner party too.

Serves 4

1 medium chicken, about 1.5kg (3lb)

1 large lemon

large sprig of sage

large sprig of rosemary

25g (1oz) butter, at room temperature

2 garlic cloves, crushed

1 tbsp olive oil

750g (1lb 10oz) floury potatoes, such as King Edward or Maris Piper

coarse sea salt and freshly ground black pepper

Step one Preheat the oven to 200°C/400°F/gas 6. Snip any strings that are binding the chicken legs, then wipe inside the cavity with kitchen paper and season. Cut the lemon into 5 or 6 pieces and push them into the cavity with the sage and rosemary sprigs.

Step two Mix together the butter and garlic with some salt and pepper. Loosen the skin on the breast, then using your fingers spread the butter between the flesh and the skin. Pull the skin back into place. Place the bird in a large roasting tin and brush all over with a little oil and a sprinkling of coarse salt. Roast for 30 minutes.

Step three Meanwhile, peel and cube the potatoes, then cook them in a pan of boiling water for exactly 5 minutes. Drain in a colander, shaking them vigorously to 'fluff up' the outside of the potatoes – this helps to give them a lovely, crunchy finish when they are roasted.

Step four Open the oven and quickly toss the potatoes into the roasting tin, shaking to coat them in the buttery chicken juices. Roast for a further 1 hour, without turning or poking, until the chicken is cooked through and golden, and the potatoes are crunchy and golden on the outside and fluffy and floury on the inside. Cut the chicken into quarters and serve with the pan juices and roasties.

Chicken and Broccoli Gratin

This recipe is great for using up leftover roast chicken, but a shop-bought cooked chicken also works well.

Step one Preheat the oven to 190°C/375°F/gas 5. Strip the meat off the bones of the chicken and shred or cut it into bite-sized pieces – you'll need 450g (1lb) in total. Place the stripped meat into a bowl and set aside.

Step two Blanch the broccoli in a pan of boiling, salted water for 2–3 minutes, then drain and refresh under cold running water. Tip onto kitchen paper to drain completely.

Step three Heat the béchamel sauce in a large pan and whisk in the stock and cream. Bring to a simmer, then cook for a few minutes, stirring occasionally, until you have achieved a thick pouring sauce. You should have about 600ml (1 pint) in total. Season to taste.

Step four Grease a shallow ovenproof dish. Melt the butter in a small pan, add the onion and sauté for a few minutes, then stir in the breadcrumbs and herbs and season to taste. Arrange the chicken and broccoli in the prepared dish and spoon the sauce over to cover them completely. Sprinkle the breadcrumb mixture on top and bake for 20 minutes until bubbling and golden brown. Serve at once with some crusty bread.

Serves 4

1 cooked chicken (to give you 450g/1lb meat)

450g (1lb) broccoli, cut into florets

450ml (¾ pint) béchamel or cheese sauce (home-made or bought)

150ml (¼ pint) chicken stock

4 tbsp double cream or crème fraîche

25g (1oz) butter, plus extra for greasing

1 small onion, finely chopped

75g (3oz) fresh white breadcrumbs

leaves from ½ x 20g (¾oz) packet fresh flat-leaf parsley, chopped

2–3 fresh sage leaves, finely chopped

salt and freshly ground black pepper

crusty bread, to serve

Chicken Parmigiana with Parsley-butter Tagliatelle

This classic Italian dish can easily be prepared in advance and cooked just before serving.

Serves 4

1 tbsp olive oil

1 garlic clove, crushed

1 x 400g (14oz) tin chopped tomatoes

1 tbsp tomato purée

leaves from 1 x 20g (¾oz) packet fresh basil, chopped

50g (2oz) Parmesan, finely grated

25g (1oz) seasoned plain flour

1 egg, beaten

25g (1oz) butter

4 boneless, skinless chicken breasts

150g (5oz) mozzarella, sliced

salt and freshly ground black pepper

for the parsley butter tagliatelle

350g (12oz) egg tagliatelle

25g (1oz) butter

1 small garlic clove, crushed

leaves from 1 x 20g (¾oz) packet fresh flat-leaf parsley, chopped

Step one Preheat the oven to 200°C/400°F/gas 6. Put the olive oil and garlic into a medium-sized pan and, as soon as it starts to sizzle, add the tomatoes and tomato purée. Simmer for about 10 minutes until thickened. Stir in the basil and some seasoning to taste. Set to one side.

Step two Mix half the grated Parmesan into the seasoned flour and tip it into a shallow dish. Tip the egg into a separate shallow dish.

Step three Melt the butter in a medium-sized frying pan. Dip the chicken breasts into the beaten egg, then the flour and cheese mixture and add them to the pan. Cook over a medium–high heat for about 3 minutes on each side until lightly golden. Transfer them to a small, shallow ovenproof dish and pour over the tomato sauce.

Step four Lay two slices of mozzarella on top of each chicken breast and sprinkle over the rest of the Parmesan. Cover the dish loosely with foil and bake for 15 minutes. Uncover and cook for a further 15 minutes or until the cheese is lightly browned.

Step five Meanwhile, bring a large pan of salted water to the boil. Add the tagliatelle and cook for 8–9 minutes. Mix the butter with the garlic, chopped parsley and some seasoning to taste. Drain the pasta, return to the pan with the parsley butter and toss together well.

Step six Remove the chicken from the oven and serve with the tagliatelle, garnished with a few leaves of flat-leaf parsley.

Chicken, Pepper and Brie Puff Parcels

Use chicken breasts that each weigh about 175g (6oz) for these parcels, or there won't be enough to wrap around the cheese and peppers once they've been flattened.

Serves 2

2 boneless, skinless chicken breasts

2 tsp olive oil

1 tsp lemon juice

leaves from 2 large sprigs of thyme

1 red pepper

50g (2oz) ripe Brie, thinly sliced

1 x 500g (1lb 2oz) pack chilled puff pastry

1 egg, beaten, to glaze

1 tbsp finely grated Parmesan cheese

salt and freshly ground black pepper

Step one Put each chicken breast, skinned-side down, onto a large sheet of clingfilm and fold back the little fillets. Cover with another sheet of clingfilm and bash with a rolling pin to flatten, giving it a bit more of a bash on the thicker side, until the breast is about the size of a large saucer. Mix the olive oil, lemon juice, thyme leaves, salt and pepper in a shallow dish. Add the chicken, turn once and marinate for at least 1 hour.

Step two Preheat the oven to 220°C/425°F/gas 7. Roast the pepper for 20 minutes, then remove and leave to cool. Break in half and remove the stalk, skin and seeds. Remove the chicken from the marinade, place half the pepper on one side of each piece and fold over the other side.

Step three Heat a dry, non-stick frying pan, add the chicken and pepper 'sandwiches' and fry for 1–1½ minutes on each side until lightly browned. Remove and leave to cool slightly, then slip the sliced Brie in with the red pepper.

Step four Cut the pastry block in half and roll out each piece on a lightly floured surface. Cut out two 25cm (10in) discs. Place a stuffed chicken breast in the centre of each pastry disc. Brush the edge of the disc with beaten egg and bring the sides together over the top of the chicken. Press together firmly to seal the ends well, then fold them back on themselves to make an even better seal. Place on a greased baking sheet and chill for at least 20 minutes.

Step five Preheat the oven to 200°C/400°F/gas 6. Brush the parcels with beaten egg, sprinkle the tops with the cheese and bake for 30 minutes until crisp and golden.

Roasted Blackened Chicken Chichen Itza

A classic dish, traditionally barbecued, which is probably as old as the famous ancient pyramid of Chichen Itza in southern Mexico. I really like this recipe because the dry rub on the skin of the chicken blackens to a tasty, crunchy coating during cooking, leaving the flesh inside moist and juicy. How do you like yours?

Serves 4

2 garlic cloves, crushed

1 tbsp freshly ground black pepper

1 tsp dried oregano

1 tsp dried thyme

1 tbsp paprika

1 tbsp caster sugar

2 tsp crushed dried chilli

1 tsp English mustard powder

1 tsp salt

1 medium chicken, 1–1.2kg (2¼–2½ lb), quartered

olive oil, for drizzling

salad and jacket potatoes, to serve

Step one Mix the garlic, pepper, oregano, thyme, paprika, sugar, chilli, mustard powder and salt together in a large, shallow dish. Roll the chicken quarters in the spice mixture and leave for 5–10 minutes.

Step two Preheat the oven to 200°C/400°F/gas 6 and heat a roasting tin. Place the chicken in the hot roasting tin, drizzle over a little olive oil and roast for 40–45 minutes until the skin is slightly charred and the meat is cooked through. Alternatively, barbecue the chicken over medium-hot coals for 30–45 minutes, turning occasionally.

Step three Serve with jacket potatoes and a nice salad.

Bang-bang Chicken with Vegetable Ribbon Salad

I first tried this dish many moons ago at Le Caprice, the famous London restaurant that originally brought it to people's attention, and where it's a favourite to this day.

Step one Preheat the oven to 200°C/400°F/gas 6. Rub each chicken breast with the olive oil, season and roast in the oven for 35–40 minutes until the chicken is tender. Remove from the oven and set aside to cool to room temperature.

Step two Now make the dressing. Place all the ingredients in a glass bowl that will fit snugly on top of a small pan of simmering water. Do not allow the bottom of the bowl to touch the water. Stir over the heat until the dressing is smooth. Remove from the heat and keep warm.

Step three Using a vegetable peeler, cut the cucumber and carrots into long ribbons. Slice the salad onions. Mix together the cucumber, carrots, salad onions and beansprouts. Divide the salad among four plates.

Step four Shred the chicken and arrange on top of the salad. Drizzle over the dressing, scatter the peanuts and sesame seeds (if using) on top and serve immediately with any extra dressing served alongside.

If you'd like to poach rather than roast the chicken breasts, cover them with water and add some sliced onion, garlic, fresh root ginger and a few peppercorns. The resulting stock can be used to make a lovely soup.

Serves 4

4 boneless, skinless chicken breasts

2 tbsp olive oil

1 cucumber

3 medium carrots, peeled

4 salad onions

50g (2oz) beansprouts

75g (3oz) dry-roasted peanuts, chopped

1 tbsp toasted sesame seeds (optional)

for the dressing

100g (4oz) smooth peanut butter

3 tbsp toasted sesame oil

2 tbsp sunflower or groundnut oil

2 tbsp chilli sauce

1 tbsp soy sauce

1 tbsp rice vinegar or lime juice

1 garlic clove, crushed

Chicken, Ham and Mushroom Crusty Puff Pies

I'm always disappointed and sometimes frustrated when I taste shop-bought pies, because the meat is invariably thin and stringy and the pastry all too often soggy. So here's a lovely, moist pie that has bite and light, crisp pastry. If pushed for time, you could use a ready-made carbonara or cheese and mushroom sauce.

Serves 4

150g (5oz) button mushrooms, thickly sliced

25g (1oz) butter

4 skinless, cooked chicken breasts

100g (4oz) lean ham

350g (12oz) fresh or shop-bought cheese sauce

100g (4oz) frozen peas, thawed

1 tbsp chopped fresh parsley or tarragon

1 tbsp plain flour, for dusting

300g (11oz) puff pastry

2 tbsp milk

salt and freshly ground black pepper

Step one Preheat the oven to 200°C/400°F/gas 6. Melt the butter in a frying pan, add the sliced mushrooms and sauté over a medium-to-high heat for 3–4 minutes until tender. Tip into a large bowl.

Step two Cut the chicken into chunks and roughly chop the ham. Pour the sauce over the mushrooms and ham, add the chicken, ham, peas and parsley or tarragon. Season, mix well and divide among four individual pie dishes. Brush the edges of each dish with a little cold water.

Step three Lightly dust a work surface with the flour and roll out the pastry. Cut out four discs slightly larger than the pie dishes. Cover the dishes with the pastry discs, pressing down the edges to seal. Cut a hole for the steam to escape. Brush the tops with the milk, then place the dishes on a baking sheet and bake on the middle shelf of the oven for about 20 minutes until the pies are piping hot and golden brown. Serve immediately with steamed broccoli.

Oven-baked Harissa Chicken with Cumin Sweet Potatoes

When I visited Marrakech, I was really impressed with its vibrant spice markets and the hospitality of the shopkeepers, who were forever giving me heavenly scented sweet mint tea. There were also lots of stalls selling hot food, and the smells wafting through the air gave me such an appetite. I hope this aromatic recipe captures a little of that for you. Harissa is a Moroccan chilli paste, which is now available in most supermarkets.

Serves 4

4 chicken breasts, skin on

4 tsp harissa paste

2 tbsp olive oil

2 large sweet potatoes

1 tsp cumin seeds

2 tsp grated fresh root ginger

4 tbsp mayonnaise

1 garlic clove, crushed

salt and freshly ground black pepper

lime wedges, to serve

Step one Slash the skin of each chicken breast four or five times and place in a bowl with the harissa and 1 tablespoon of the oil. Mix to coat the chicken thoroughly, then season, cover and set aside to marinate for 10–15 minutes.

Step two Preheat the oven to 220°C/425°F/gas 7. Meanwhile, peel the sweet potatoes and cut into slices about 1cm (½in) thick. Mix with the cumin seeds, ginger and remaining oil. Season and place on a large, foil-lined baking sheet in a single layer. Bake on the upper shelf of the oven for 20 minutes.

Step three Mix together the mayonnaise and garlic. Cover and set aside.

Step four Turn the sweet potato slices over and add the chicken breasts, skin-side up, to the baking sheet. Cook for a further 25–30 minutes until the chicken is cooked through and the sweet potatoes are tender and browned at the edges. Serve immediately with steamed spring greens, a dollop of garlic mayonnaise for each portion and lime wedges to squeeze over.

Roast Juicy Chicken Thighs with Parsley and Onion Stuffing

This could quite easily be a cheat's succulent roast chicken dinner. To complete the meal, parboil a couple of small potatoes per person and toss in a little oil and butter before tucking them around the stuffed chicken thighs to roast. Cook some frozen peas just before serving and you've got a great meal with very little effort.

Serves 4

25g (1oz) butter, plus extra for greasing

1 small onion, finely chopped

50g (2oz) fresh white breadcrumbs

1 tbsp chopped fresh flat-leaf parsley

8 boneless chicken thighs, well trimmed

sea salt and freshly ground black pepper

Step one Preheat the oven to 180°C/350°F/gas 4. Melt the butter in a pan and sauté the onion for 3–4 minutes until softened. Add the breadcrumbs and parsley to the pan, stir and season to taste. Divide the stuffing among the chicken thighs and fold over to enclose, securing each one with wooden cocktail sticks to prevent them from popping open when cooking.

Step two Butter a small roasting tin and arrange the stuffed chicken thighs in it, then season the skins generously. Roast for 30–35 minutes, basting halfway through the cooking time, until the skin is crisp and golden and the thighs are cooked through and tender. Arrange the roast chicken thighs on warmed plates and serve at once.

For a video masterclass on how to tell if your chicken is cooked, go to www.mykitchentable.co.uk/videos/cookingchicken

KITCHEN
TABLE

Roast Chicken Breasts with Spiced Green Chilli Butter

For a milder flavour, replace the chilli with two crushed garlic cloves.

Step one Preheat the oven to 200°C/400°F/gas 6. Place the butter in a bowl, beat in the fresh coriander and chopped green chilli and season.

Step two Make three 0.5cm (¼in) slashes on each chicken breast. Place in a roasting tin, skin-side up. Press the spiced butter into the slashes and squeeze over the lemon juice.

Step three Roast for 35–40 minutes until completely tender and the skin is crisp and golden. Garnish with coriander and serve.

Serves 4

50g (2oz) butter, softened

2 tbsp chopped fresh coriander, plus extra to garnish

1 mild green chilli, seeded and finely chopped

4 x 175g (6oz) part-boned chicken breasts, skin on

juice of ½ lemon

sea salt and freshly ground black pepper

Clever Cook's Roast Chicken Dinner

We all have to be pretty crafty in the kitchen at times, and this speedy dinner of roast chicken, honeyed potatoes, bacon-wrapped sausages, stir-fried broccoli and bread sauce has got me out of hot water on more than one occasion. Y'know that lunch invitation you booked weeks ago but forgot about, until the unexpected Sunday 12pm phonecall – 'We're on our way'? Help!

Serves 2

4 x 100g (4oz) potatoes, each halved lengthways

2 x 100g (4oz) boneless chicken breasts

large knob of butter

2 rashers smoked streaky bacon

4 chipolata sausages

1 small onion, finely chopped

150ml (¼ pint) milk

40g (1½ oz) fresh white breadcrumbs

pinch of grated nutmeg

1 tbsp clear honey

2 tbsp olive oil

1 garlic clove, thinly sliced

200g (7oz) broccoli florets

salt and freshly ground black pepper

snipped chives, to garnish

Step one Preheat the oven to 220°C/425°F/gas 7. Cook the potatoes in a large pan of boiling, salted water for 10–15 minutes until just tender.

Step two Meanwhile, place the chicken breasts in a roasting tin, season well and dot with a little butter. Roast for 25 minutes until golden brown and cooked through. While the chicken is cooking, stretch the bacon with the back of a knife and cut each rasher in half widthways. Wrap a half rasher around each chipolata and add to the chicken pan.

Step three Heat the remaining butter in a small pan and cook the onion for 3–4 minutes until softened, then pour in the milk and bring to the boil. Lower the heat, stir in the breadcrumbs and nutmeg; season to taste and keep warm.

Step four Drain the potatoes and return them to the pan. Toss with the honey and 1 tablespoon of the oil, then arrange around the chicken in the roasting tin. Return to the oven to roast for 8–10 minutes until golden brown.

Step five Heat the remaining oil in a wok and stir-fry the garlic and broccoli for 2 minutes. Add a splash of water and cook for a further 2 minutes until tender. Season to taste. Place the chicken breasts on large serving plates with the honeyed potatoes, bacon-wrapped sausages and stir-fried broccoli. Add a spoonful of bread sauce to each plate and sprinkle with chives to garnish.

Mozzarella-oozing Rosemary Chicken

This is based on a Neapolitan dish. Lots of people think that rosemary was made for lamb, but it goes equally well with chicken. In fact, I think this will get you the 'ooh!' approval. Use fresh rosemary if you like, making the quantity up to 2 teaspoons of the chopped herb.

Step one Preheat the grill to high. Cut the mozzarella in half widthways, then cut each half into four wedges. Mix the rosemary and chilli with salt and pepper in a bowl, then toss the cheese in it.

Step two Lay the chicken thighs out flat, sprinkle with the flour and place a cheese wedge in the centre of each. Roll the chicken round the cheese and secure with wooden cocktail sticks, tucking in the ends, if possible. Place in a roasting tin, brush with oil and season. Grill for 20 minutes, turning occasionally, until cooked through.

Step three Meanwhile, cook the potatoes in a pan of boiling, salted water for 10–15 minutes until tender; drain well and keep warm. Melt the butter in a frying pan and stir-fry the leek for 3–4 minutes until softened. Mash the potatoes with the milk or cream, then stir in the leeks and season to taste.

Step four Divide the leek mash among four serving plates. Remove the cocktail sticks from the chicken and place on top. Spoon round the chicken-pan juices and serve.

Serves 4

150g (5oz) mozzarella, drained

1½ tsp dried rosemary

¼ tsp crushed dried chilli

8 boneless chicken thighs

1 tbsp plain flour

olive oil, for brushing

700g (1lb 9oz) potatoes, cubed

25g (1oz) butter

1 leek, cut into ½ cm (¼ in) coins

2 tbsp milk or single cream

salt and freshly ground black pepper

Sticky Garlic Chicken Skewers

On a hot summer's day there's nothing better than these spicy chicken skewers sizzling away on the barbie. Make up the marinade the night before, add the chicken and leave overnight – it'll give you time to relax with your guests. If the weather's not on your side, simply cook the chicken under the grill.

Serves 4

3 garlic cloves, crushed

2 tbsp clear honey

4 tbsp tomato ketchup

4 tbsp Worcestershire sauce

2 tsp English mustard

2 tsp Tabasco sauce

3 boneless, skinless chicken breasts, cut into thin strips

salt and freshly ground black pepper

salad and baby new potatoes, to serve

Step one Mix together the garlic, honey, ketchup, Worcestershire sauce, mustard and Tabasco in a non-metallic dish and season with salt and freshly ground black pepper. Toss in the chicken and stir until well combined, then cover and leave to marinate for 20–30 minutes or overnight.

Step two Soak twelve 25cm (10in) bamboo skewers in water for at least 20 minutes.

Step three Preheat the grill to high. Thread the marinated chicken onto the skewers, arrange on a foil-lined baking sheet and grill for 6–7 minutes, turning occasionally until the chicken is well browned and cooked through, or cook over the hot coals of a barbecue for 5–6 minutes. Serve with mixed salad and baby new potatoes.

Chargrilled Pineapple Chicken Pockets

Now here's a delicious low-fat fruity chicken feast. Sometimes when you combine certain foods and they work well together the finished dish is a real delight. Chicken and pineapple work beautifully together, especially with the added flavour of salad onions.

Step one Preheat the grill to medium. Cut a small shallow pocket into the side of the thickest part of each chicken breast.

Step two Drain the pineapple and reserve the juice. Finely chop the pineapple (or blitz it in a food-processor) and mix with the salad onions and a little salt and pepper. Spoon the mixture into the pockets, but do not overfill them. Secure with short, thin metal skewers or wooden cocktail sticks. If using cocktail sticks, first soak them in water for 20 minutes.

Step three Mix the reserved pineapple juice and sugar together in a small pan and leave over a low heat until the sugar has dissolved. Bring the mixture to the boil and boil vigorously until it is syrupy and reduced to about 4 tablespoons. Stir in the chilli.

Step four Grill the chicken for about 10 minutes, turning now and then, until it is about half cooked. Then brush over some of the pineapple glaze and continue to cook for another 10 minutes, turning and brushing the chicken with more glaze, until it is cooked through and the skin is nice and golden. Serve with baked sweet potatoes.

Serves 6

6 large boneless, skinless chicken breasts

225g (8oz) tinned pineapple in natural juice

2–3 salad onions, thinly sliced

50g (2oz) caster sugar

pinch of chilli powder or crushed dried chilli

salt and freshly ground black pepper

baked sweet potatoes, to serve

Chicken Chilli Burgers

You can buy minced chicken easily in the shops now. However, ring the changes and try using minced turkey too – it's really lean and low in fat. Just because it's a healthy option doesn't mean the burger will be small. This burger is big on size, style and, of course, taste.

Serves 4

500g (1lb 2oz) lean minced chicken

2 garlic cloves, crushed

1 red chilli, seeded and finely chopped

1 tbsp chopped fresh mint

2 tbsp chopped fresh parsley or coriander

2 tsp Worcestershire sauce

olive oil, for brushing

salt and freshly ground black pepper

to serve

burger buns

wild rocket and tomato slices

Step one Mix together the minced chicken, garlic, chilli, herbs, Worcestershire sauce and plenty of salt and pepper.

Step two Shape the mixture into four even-sized burgers, then brush them lightly with the oil. Preheat the grill to medium.

Step three Grill for 5 minutes on each side – or cook on a medium-hot barbecue – until well browned and cooked through. Serve in burger buns with rocket and juicy, sliced tomatoes.

Have you made this recipe? Tell us what you think at
www.mykitchentable.co.uk/blog

KITCHEN
TABLE

128

Fennel and Lemon Barbecue Chicken Drumsticks

The most popular method of flavouring food for barbecuing is the marinade. Marinades are mostly oil-based mixtures used to flavour and tenderize fish and meats prior to cooking and to help keep them moist during cooking. This marinade is ideal for delicately flavoured chicken, white fish and seafood. Fennel herb is not always easy to come by, so just substitute another herb with a slightly aniseed flavour such as tarragon or basil if need be.

step one Mix together the ingredients for the marinade and pour into a shallow dish. Add the chicken legs, coating them thoroughly and leave them to marinade for 2 hours (or up to 48 hours in the fridge), turning every now and then to make sure they're covered.

step two Bring the chicken back to room temperature if it's been chilled. Heat the barbecue. Scrape off the excess marinade and barbecue on medium-hot coals for 20–25 minutes.

It is very important not to overdo the oil in a marinade as this is what causes a barbecue to flare up, resulting in that well-known blackened barbecue look.

Serves 4

1 tbsp fennel seeds, crushed

3 tbsp fresh fennel herb, tarragon or basil, chopped

finely grated zest and juice of 1 small lemon

4 tbsp olive oil

2 garlic cloves, crushed

salt and freshly ground black pepper

8 chicken legs

Buffalo Chicken Wings with Blue Cheese Dip

Chicken wings make a great pre-feast nibble and this is a tasty way of turning what is often thought of as an off-cut into something scrumptious.

Serves 6

24 large chicken wings

2 celery hearts, cut into chunky sticks

for the sauce

1 onion, finely chopped

1 garlic clove, crushed

40g (1½ oz) butter

1 tbsp light soft brown sugar

2 tsp English mustard powder

2 tsp chilli powder

250ml (8fl oz) tomato ketchup

120ml (4fl oz) red wine vinegar

1 tbsp Worcestershire sauce

for the dip

100g (4oz) Danish Blue

1 garlic clove, crushed

3 tbsp mayonnaise

1 tbsp lemon juice

2 tbsp finely chopped onion

4 tbsp soured cream

a little chopped fresh parsley, to garnish

Step one For the blue cheese dip, put the cheese, garlic, mayonnaise and lemon juice into a food-processor and blend until smooth. Stir in the chopped onion and soured cream. Spoon the mixture into a bowl, sprinkle with the chopped parsley and set aside in the fridge until needed.

Step two For the sauce, fry the onion and garlic in the butter for 5 minutes until soft. Add the rest of the sauce ingredients and simmer for 3 minutes until thickened. Keep warm.

Step three Cut the tips off the chicken wings, then thread them onto parallel pairs of long, flat metal skewers, so that they rest across each pair of skewers like the rungs of a ladder. This makes it easier to turn them during cooking. Barbecue the wings over medium-hot coals for 20–25 minutes, turning regularly, until golden.

Step four Slide the wings off the skewers into the pot of sauce and toss together well. Lift them out onto a plate and serve with the dip and celery sticks.

Spiced Buttered Barbecued Chicken

This recipe can be used for large poussins, guinea fowl or small chickens, especially the corn-fed ones. You will just need to adjust the cooking times, allowing about 15 minutes per 450g (1lb) plus 15 minutes. You must have a covered barbecue for this recipe.

Step one Remove the elastic from the legs of the chicken, and any giblets and excess fat from the chicken cavities.

Step two Mix the paprika, curry powder, ground cloves and cinnamon, lemon zest, garlic, chopped coriander, salt and some black pepper with the butter to make a smooth paste.

Step three Loosen the skin over the breast of the chicken and spread about half of the curry butter over the breast meat in a thin layer. Spread the rest of the butter inside the cavity of the chicken, then push in the bay leaves. Tie the legs back together with string and leave to stand for at least 1 hour.

Step four Prepare your barbecue for the indirect method of cooking: if using a coal barbecue, scrape the coals to opposite sides of the hearth; for a gas barbecue turn off the middle burner closest to the food. Place the chicken on the rack directly over the tray, cover with the lid and cook for about 1 hour until the juices run clear when the thickest part of the thigh is pierced with a thin metal skewer.

Serves 4

1 x 1.5kg (3lb)
corn-fed chicken

1 tsp paprika

1 tbsp mild
curry powder

pinch of ground cloves

pinch of ground
cinnamon

finely grated zest
of ½ lemon

1 garlic clove, crushed

1 tbsp chopped
fresh coriander

½ tsp salt

50g (2oz) butter,
softened

2 fresh bay leaves

freshly ground black
pepper

Chicken Sage and Red Onion Brochettes

Brochette is just a fancy name for a kebab, and these juicy skewers well deserve a snazzy title.

Serves 4

8 boneless chicken thighs

16 fresh sage leaves

2 small red onions, each cut into 8 wedges

3 tbsp olive oil

1 tsp balsamic vinegar

2 garlic cloves, crushed

⅛ tsp crushed dried chilli

salt and freshly ground black pepper

to serve

salad leaves

bruschetta-style bread

Step one Quarter each chicken thigh and thread, skin-side out, onto 8 metal skewers, alternating each piece with a sage leaf or red onion wedge.

Step two Whisk together the olive oil, balsamic vinegar, garlic, chilli and plenty of salt and pepper. Brush the mixture over the brochettes and cook over medium-low coals or under a preheated grill for 20–30 minutes, turning occasionally, until the chicken is crusty and dark golden and the red onions are sweet and softened.

Step three Serve on a bed of salad leaves with crunchy bruschetta-style bread.

Munchy Mustard Chicken Escalopes

The idea of this dish is to cover a chunk of toasted ciabatta with baby leaf salad, add a piece of grilled chicken escalope and finish off with a good dollop of mustard mayonnaise. Delicious! Happy munching.

Serves 4

4 large boneless, skinless chicken breasts

4 tbsp olive oil

2–3 tbsp Dijon mustard

1 garlic clove, crushed

1 ciabatta loaf

1 tsp lemon juice

snipped fresh chives, to garnish

salt and freshly ground black pepper

for the salad

50g (2oz) baby spinach leaves

1 bunch watercress, large stalks removed

½ small radicchio

4 tbsp mayonnaise

1 tbsp Dijon mustard

Step one Place the chicken breasts one at a time between two large sheets of cling film and beat out gently with a rolling pin until they are about 0.5cm (¼in) thick and have almost doubled in size.

Step two Mix 3 tablespoons of the oil with the mustard and crushed garlic. Brush some of this mixture over both sides of the chicken, season with salt and pepper and set to one side.

Step three For the salad, place the prepared leaves in a bowl and lightly toss together. Mix the mayonnaise with the mustard. Set aside with the salad.

Step four Cut the ciabatta in half lengthways as if you were going to make a sandwich and then across to make four chunky pieces. Place cut-side down on the barbecue and leave for a couple of minutes until lightly toasted. Remove and set aside.

Step five Barbecue the chicken over medium-hot coals for about 3 minutes on each side until golden on the outside but still juicy in the centre.

Step six Whisk the rest of the olive oil, the lemon juice and some salt and pepper into the remaining mustard mixture. Add to the salad leaves and toss together lightly.

Step seven Place a piece of ciabatta on each plate and spread over a little mustard mayonnaise. Sprinkle over a few leaves, then put the chicken on top, followed by more leaves. Add another dollop of the mustard mayonnaise and sprinkle with a few snipped chives. Serve the awaiting munchers.

Barbecued Chicken and Bacon Rolls

This is a very simple barbecue dish that can be prepared well in advance. You can vary the fillings very easily – those pick-and-mix portions of cheese from the supermarket are just the right size for one chicken breast. Oooh, now that sounds nice!

Serves 6

6 boneless, skinless chicken breasts

2 tbsp tomato ketchup

6 Lincolnshire sausages, skinned

6 rashers rindless back bacon

Step one Place the chicken breasts one at a time between two large sheets of clingfilm and flatten very slightly with a rolling pin. Spread the underside of each piece with the tomato ketchup, then lay one of the sausages across the fatter end of each breast.

Step two Fold the chicken around the sausage, then wrap each one in a rasher of bacon and secure in place with a fine metal trussing skewer or wooden cocktail stick. (If using cocktail sticks, soak them in cold water for 30 minutes beforehand.)

Step three Barbecue over medium-hot coals, turning now and then, for about 25 minutes until golden. Remove the skewers or cocktail sticks before serving.

For a bit of variety, stuff the chicken with different flavoured sausages, replace the tomato ketchup with mustard, or leave out the tomato ketchup and instead of sausages use 25g (1oz) sticks of coarse pork pâté or cheese such as Cheddar, Gruyère or Danish Blue. You could also spread the chicken with pesto and stuff it with a couple of basil leaves and a 25g (1oz) stick of mozzarella.

Chunky Chicken and Bacon Burgers

Home-made burgers are a doddle to make, and it's easy to vary the flavours, too. For an extra-tasty but more calorific burger, serve with extra grilled bacon and a dollop of blue-cheese mayonnaise.

Step one Mix all the ingredients for the burger together in a bowl or blitz quickly in a food processor until the meat starts to hold together.

Step two Divide the mixture into four and shape into 10cm (4in) flat discs, either by hand or by pressing the mixture into a metal pastry cutter.

Step three Brush the burgers with a little oil and barbecue over medium-hot coals for 6–7 minutes each side until well done and serve in buns with the sliced tomatoes and a few rocket leaves.

Serves 4

680g (1½ lb) minced chicken

6 rashers rindless streaky bacon, very finely chopped

2 garlic cloves, crushed

1 small onion, finely chopped

2 tbsp double cream

1 tbsp chopped fresh parsley

salt and freshly ground black pepper

to serve

4 sesame seed rolls, halved

2 tomatoes, thinly sliced

a handful of rocket leaves

Coconut Chicken and Mango Skewers

The smell of these chicken skewers is sensational, and the orange of the mango and green of the peas make these into attractive as well as tasty kebabs, flavoured with Thai green curry paste and coconut milk. I bet you're licking your lips.

Serves 4

450g (1lb) boneless, skinless chicken breasts

1 large, ripe but firm mango

50g (2oz) mangetout (about 24)

for the marinade

120ml (4fl oz) tinned coconut milk

1 tbsp Thai green curry paste

1 tsp prepared minced lemon grass from a jar

1 tsp palm sugar or light muscovado sugar

1 tbsp Thai fish sauce

1 tbsp groundnut or sunflower oil

finely grated zest of ½ lime

1 tsp lime juice

Step one Cut the chicken into 2.5cm (1in) cubes. Mix together all the ingredients for the marinade, stir in the chicken and leave it to marinate for 2 hours at room temperature, or overnight in the fridge.

Step two Peel the mango, then slice the flesh away from either side of the thin flat stone and cut into 1cm (½in) pieces.

Step three Drop the mangetout into a pan of boiling, salted water. Bring back to the boil, then drain and refresh under running cold water. Soak eight 25cm (10in) bamboo skewers in cold water for 30 minutes.

Step four Thread three pieces of chicken and three mangetout folded around three pieces of mango alternately onto each skewer. Barbecue the skewers over medium-hot coals for 10 minutes, turning now and then and brushing with the leftover marinade, until the chicken is lightly browned.

Balinese Chicken

For this recipe, a thick spice and coconut paste is spread under the skin of the chicken instead of over the outside. This helps it to flavour the meat and prevents the tasty paste from over-browning and dropping off into the fire during cooking. Go easy when lifting the skin off the chicken and remember fingers only – no knives or you'll pierce the skin!

Step one Put the galangal or root ginger, garlic, lemongrass, chillies, turmeric, coriander, salad onions and lime leaves or lime zest into a food processor and blend to a coarse paste.

Step two Melt the creamed coconut in a small pan, stir in the paste and leave to cool slightly until thickened but not set hard.

Step three Loosen the skin of each breast with your fingers, leaving it attached along one long edge. Spread the paste over the breast meat, lift the skin back into place and secure the open edge with a skewer or cocktail stick. Barbecue the chicken over medium-hot coals for 25 minutes, turning regularly, until the skin is crisp and golden. Remove the skewers or cocktail sticks before serving.

Serves 6

5cm (2in) galangal or fresh root ginger, peeled and chopped

2 garlic cloves, crushed

1 lemon grass stalk, roughly chopped

2 red birds eye chillies, de-seeded and chopped

2 tsp ground turmeric

2 tbsp chopped fresh coriander

6 salad onions, trimmed and chopped

2 fresh kaffir lime leaves, finely shredded, or the finely grated zest of 1 lime

75g (3oz) creamed coconut

6 part-boned chicken breasts

6 fine metal trussing skewers or cocktail sticks soaked in cold water for 30 minutes

Chicken and Frankfurter Dogs with Fried Onions

Here's a twist on that well-known street food. It tastes much better too, thanks to the tangy barbecue sauce that's used to flavour the chicken and frankfurters. Kids love 'em.

Serves 4

75g (3oz) butter

1 tbsp oil

3 onions, thinly sliced

1 tsp granulated sugar

3 boneless, skinless chicken breasts

4 jumbo frankfurters

120ml (4fl oz) spicy tomato ketchup

1 tbsp English mustard

1 tbsp tomato purée

1 tbsp Worcestershire sauce

½ tsp barbecue seasoning

4 hot dog rolls

Step one Heat 25g (1oz) of the butter and the oil in a medium-sized pan. Add the onions and fry over a gentle heat for 15 minutes, stirring now and then, until very soft. Add the sugar and cook for another 15 minutes, still stirring, until they have lightly caramelised. Set aside and keep warm.

Step two While the onions are cooking, soak four 30cm (12in) bamboo skewers in cold water for 30 minutes.

Step three Cut each chicken breast lengthways into four strips, and cut each frankfurter into four pieces. Roll each piece of chicken up into a spiral. Thread three pieces of chicken and four pieces of frankfurter alternately onto each skewer.

Step four Melt the rest of the butter in a small pan. Stir in the tomato ketchup, mustard, tomato purée, Worcestershire sauce and barbecue seasoning. Brush the kebabs liberally with the sauce and barbecue over medium-hot coals for about 20 minutes, turning and basting with the leftover sauce now and then. Brush with the rest of the barbecue sauce right at the end of cooking so that the kebabs are nice and gooey.

Step five To serve, split open the hot dog rolls and spoon in some of the fried onions. Rest a kebab on top of the onions, close the bun tightly and slide out the skewers.

Flash Chicken Satay

I always serve chicken satay (the miniature variety) before we get down to the serious nosh, and the plate is empty in a flash. These scrummy skewers also make a great main course, and are delicious cooked over hot coals and served with a cold beer. You'll need to soak them in water for 20 minutes before using them.

Step one Preheat the grill to high. Now make your satay sauce. Place the coconut cream and peanut butter in a bowl and beat together until well blended. Stir in the Worcestershire sauce and Tabasco. Set the sauce aside.

Step two Put the chicken breasts between sheets of cling film, then use a rolling pin to bash them as thin as possible. Remove the clingfilm and cut each breast in half lengthways.

Step three Pour half the satay sauce into a shallow dish and add the chicken pieces, turning to coat them in the sauce. Thread the chicken onto skewers and cook under the hot grill for 4 minutes on each side until cooked through and well browned.

Step four Gently heat the remaining satay sauce in a small pan with a splash of water. Halve the lemon and squeeze the juice of one half into the warm sauce.

Step five Pile the carrot and cucumber ribbons on top of the warm naans and squeeze over the remaining lemon juice. Arrange the skewers on top and drizzle over the warm satay sauce. Scatter the peanuts on to garnish, and serve.

Serves 2

1 x 200g (7oz) carton coconut cream

4 tbsp crunchy peanut butter

1–2 tsp Worcestershire sauce

a few drops of Tabasco sauce

2 x 75g (3oz) boneless, skinless chicken breasts

1 lemon

1 carrot, cut into thin ribbons

1 mini cucumber, cut into thin ribbons

2 warm naan breads

salt and freshly ground black pepper

25g (1oz) dry-roasted peanuts, roughly chopped, to serve

Peppy's Barbecue Chicken with Jamaican Fried Dumplings

The herby fried dumplings are the perfect accompaniment to my mum's spicy barbecue chicken. For an extra kick, why not add ¼ teaspoon of crushed dried chilli to the dumpling mixture.

Serves 4

4 tbsp tomato ketchup

juice of 1 large lemon

2 tbsp soy sauce

1 tbsp soft dark brown sugar

½ tsp ground allspice (Jamaican pepper)

½ tsp cayenne pepper

½ tsp salt

4 boneless, skinless chicken breasts

mixed salad leaves dressed with olive oil and lemon juice, to serve

for the fried dumplings

200g (7oz) plain flour

1 tsp baking powder

2 tbsp finely chopped fresh parsley

½ tsp dried thyme

½ tsp salt

200ml (7fl oz) milk

vegetable oil, for deep-frying

Step one In a large bowl, mix together the ketchup, lemon juice, soy sauce, sugar, allspice, cayenne and salt. Add the chicken breasts, stirring to coat in the marinade, then cover and set aside for 20 minutes or so.

Step two Meanwhile, make the dumplings: mix together the flour, baking powder, herbs and salt. Beat in the milk to make a thick batter.

Step three Heat 5cm (2in) of oil in a wok or deep frying pan – the oil should be hot enough so that when a cube of bread is added to the pan, it browns in about 1½ minutes. Cook spoonfuls of the batter, in batches, for 3–4 minutes until puffed, golden brown and cooked through. Drain on kitchen paper.

Step four Cook the chicken on a hot barbecue or in an oiled griddle pan for 8–10 minutes on each side until well browned and cooked through. Serve with mixed salad leaves and the dumplings.

Coriander and Lime Chicken

I'm always looking for new ways of serving chicken, especially ones that are quick to make and really tasty. This dish is a real winner. I like to serve it with mushrooms, noodles and salad onions. Leftovers are great served up the next day with a salad or in a French-bread sandwich.

Step one Finely chop the garlic and coriander, then mix in the peppercorns, sugar, lime juice, fish sauce, soy sauce and sunflower oil until well blended. Place the chicken breasts in the marinade and set aside for 1–2 hours, turning from time to time.

Step two Preheat a ridged griddle pan or heavy, non-stick frying pan and cook the chicken for 7–8 minutes on each side until it is cooked through and golden brown with good bar marks. Serve hot or cold, garnished with coriander leaves.

The marinade contains lime juice, which tenderises the chicken. After more than a few hours, though, the meat fibres can become so soft that the chicken literally falls apart, which means that this dish is not suitable for overnight marinating.

Serves 4

6 garlic cloves

4 tbsp fresh coriander leaves, plus extra to garnish

2 tsp black peppercorns, coarsely ground

2 tsp caster sugar

juice of 2 limes

2 tsp Thai fish sauce (nam pla)

1 tbsp light soy sauce

1 tbsp sunflower oil

4 boneles, skinless chicken breasts

For more recipes from My Kitchen Table, sign up for our newsletter at www.mykitchentable.co.uk/newsletter

Cajun Chicken, Atchafalaya Style

Take a trip down the Atchafalaya River in Cajun country and you'll come across this classic dish. It's a must for all you spicy Cajun connoisseurs. It's simply delicious. I like to use a whole chicken cut into eight pieces for this dish, as the bones make a lovely stock, but thighs and drumsticks on the bone are just as good. The slits cut into the chicken pieces allow the sauce to penetrate for a fuller flavour, and reduce the cooking time by approximately 10 minutes.

Serves 4

150ml (¼ pint)
chicken stock

250ml (8fl oz) tomato
ketchup

100g (4oz) soft light
brown sugar

1 tbsp hot chilli sauce

1 tbsp soy sauce

1 tbsp Worcestershire
sauce

1 onion, finely
chopped

4 garlic cloves,
crushed

1 tsp paprika

2 tsp crushed
dried chilli

2 tbsp red wine
vinegar

1 medium chicken,
1–1.2kg (2¼–2½ lb),
cut into 8 pieces

2 tbsp olive oil

chips, to serve

Step one Make a barbecue sauce by combining the chicken stock, tomato ketchup, sugar, chilli sauce, soy sauce, Worcestershire sauce, onion, garlic, paprika, chilli flakes and vinegar in a small pan and simmering gently for 20 minutes.

Step two Cut three or four slits in each chicken piece and brush them with the oil, then spoon over half the barbecue sauce, rubbing it into the slits and coating the chicken well.

Step three Cook under a medium-hot grill on the lower shelf, or over medium-hot coals on the barbie, for 30–45 minutes, turning occasionally, until the chicken is dark, glossy and cooked through. Serve with freshly fried chips and the remaining sauce drizzled over the chicken pieces.

Jamaican Jerk Chicken

This classic Jamaican jerk chicken is the perfect way to enjoy chicken without adding lots of fat. Be careful with the habañeros or Scotch bonnet chillies used in the marinade, as they are extremely hot – some say the hottest in the world. Don't tell my dad – he eats them for breakfast!

Step one Put all the ingredients, except for the chicken, into a food-processor and whizz until smooth.

Step two Put the chicken in a large, shallow non-metallic dish and pour over the sauce. Cover with clingfilm and leave to marinate in the fridge for 24 hours, turning the chicken every now and then. If you've not got time to marinate overnight, cut some deep grooves into the chicken to allow the spices to penetrate the chicken more quickly, and marinate for a few hours before cooking.

Step three Preheat the grill to medium. Grill the chicken for 25–30 minutes – or barbecue over medium coals – basting now and then with the leftover sauce. Alternatively, you can bake the chicken pieces on a baking sheet in a medium-hot oven (200°C/400°F/gas 6) for 25–30 minutes. As the chicken cooks, the thickened sauce will go quite black in places, but as it falls off it will leave behind lovely, tender, moist jerk meat beneath.

Step four Serve with rice, chillies and shredded salad onions for the perfect flavour combination.

Serves 6

225g (8oz) onions, quartered

2 habañeros or Scotch bonnet chillies, halved and seeded

5cm (2in) piece of fresh root ginger, roughly chopped

½ tsp ground allspice

leaves from 15g (½ oz) fresh thyme sprigs

1 tsp freshly ground black pepper

120ml (4fl oz) white wine vinegar

120ml (4fl oz) dark soy sauce

6 large skinless chicken pieces

rice, chillies and shredded salad onions, to serve

Gorgeous Chicken Korma

My chicken korma is based on a spicy, creamy dish from Kashmir.
It's incredibly easy to make and very, very tasty. Chicken korma is
popular because the flavours blend together perfectly, leaving that
gorgeous taste lingering on your tastebuds until the next mouthful.

Serves 4

1 tbsp vegetable oil

1 onion, roughly chopped

350ml (12fl oz) natural yoghurt

200ml (7fl oz) double cream

25g (1oz) butter

½ tsp salt

1 tsp ground turmeric

2 tsp hot chilli powder

3 garlic cloves, crushed

3 tbsp ground almonds

4 x 100g (4oz) boneless, skinless chicken breasts, each cut into 6 pieces

toasted flaked almonds and fresh coriander sprigs, to garnish (optional)

naan bread or rice, and cucumber, to serve

Step one Preheat the oven to 200°C/400°F/gas 6. Heat the oil
in a small pan and cook the onion for 5 minutes until softened.
Place in a food-processor with the yoghurt, cream, butter, salt,
turmeric, chilli, garlic and almonds and whizz until well blended.

Step two Arrange the chicken in a greased ovenproof dish
and pour over the korma mixture. Bake for 30 minutes until
the chicken is cooked through. Spoon onto plates, garnish with
flaked almonds and coriander sprigs, if you wish, and serve
with naan or rice, and cucumber.

*If you have time, allow the chicken to marinate in the korma
sauce for up to 2 hours before cooking.*

SOS Chicken Curry with Pilau Rice

If you have little time on your hands but want a truly lovely meal and you don't mind using the odd ready-prepared ingredient, look no further – this dish is for you. Look out for reduced-fat ready-cooked chicken tikka fillets, as these are much lower in fat than standard chicken tikka. A garnish of coriander adds freshness, but isn't essential.

Step one Place the passata in a small pan, stir in the curry paste and heat gently.

Step two Meanwhile, for the rice, heat the oil in a wok and stir-fry the onion for 4 minutes until nicely browned. Stir in the rice, turmeric and raisins and heat gently for 3–4 minutes, adding a splash of water if the mixture is a little dry.

Step three Add the chicken and yoghurt to the tomato mixture, bring to the boil and simmer for 2 minutes until warmed through. Stir in the sugar and season to taste.

Step four Season the rice and divide among serving plates. Spoon over the chicken mixture and garnish with coriander, if using.

Serves 6

1 x 500g (1lb 2oz) carton passata

1–2 tbsp hot curry paste

400g (14oz) cooked boneless tandoori or tikka chicken breasts, cut into bite-sized pieces

150ml (¼ pint) 0% fat Greek yoghurt

½ tsp caster sugar

salt and freshly ground black pepper

chopped fresh coriander, to garnish (optional)

for the rice

2 tsp vegetable oil

1 onion, sliced

675g (1½lb) cooked white rice

1 tsp ground turmeric

25g (1oz) seedless raisins

Chicken in a Pot with Lemon and Thyme Dumplings

You can't go far wrong with this delicious one-pot supper. It has loads of flavour, appeals to all the family and takes little time to prepare compared to traditional casseroles.

Serves 4

2 tbsp olive oil

3 boneless, skinless chicken breasts, cut into strips

1 onion, sliced

2 garlic cloves, crushed

2 carrots, cut into chunky slices

2 leeks, trimmed and sliced

120ml (4floz) white wine

3 fresh thyme sprigs

900ml (1½ pints) chicken stock

1 x 400g (14oz) tin cannellini beans, drained and rinsed

salt and freshly ground black pepper

for the dumplings

100g (4oz) plain flour

1 tsp baking powder

2 tsp chopped fresh thyme leaves

grated zest of 1 lemon

50g (2oz) shredded suet

120ml (4floz) cold water

Step one Heat the oil in a large pan with a lid. Add the chicken, season generously and cook on a fairly high heat for 2 minutes until browned all over. Add the onion and garlic and continue to fry for another 2 minutes until the onion has softened slightly but not coloured, stirring occasionally.

Step two Tip the carrots and leeks into the pan, pour in the wine and add the thyme, allowing the wine to reduce for 1 minute over a high heat. Stir in the stock, then simmer for 10 minutes until the vegetables are tender and the liquid has slightly reduced. Season to taste.

Step three Meanwhile, make the dumplings. Place the flour in a bowl and add the baking powder, thyme, lemon zest and a pinch of salt. Stir in the suet then gradually add the cold water until the mixture forms a soft dough. Divide the dough into eight and, with lightly floured hands, shape into balls.

Step four Stir the cannellini beans into the casserole and sit the dumplings on the top. Cover and simmer for a further 10 minutes until the dumplings have slightly puffed up and cooked through. Check the seasoning. To serve, ladle the chicken mixture into warmed serving bowls and top each with a couple of dumplings.

Flambé Tequila Chicken with Pine Nuts

For those evenings when you want the food to reflect the mood and yet you want to be involved in the party instead of being stuck in the kitchen, this boozy little number could be right up your street.

Step one Heat a small frying pan and toast the pine nuts for 2–3 minutes until golden. Remove from the pan and set aside.

Step two Heat 2 tablespoons of the oil in a large, heavy-based pan with a lid. Add the chicken and cook over a moderate heat for about 6 minutes, turning once, then remove from the pan and set aside.

Step three Add the remaining oil to the pan and gently fry the onion and garlic for 3–4 minutes until softened but not coloured, stirring occasionally. Add 2 tablespoons of the tequila and carefully flambé the ingredients in the pan (see below). Stir in the tomato purée, chopped tomatoes, Tabasco, paprika and sugar and cook for a few minutes.

Step four Pour in the stock and return the chicken to the pan. Cover and simmer for a further 10 minutes until the chicken is tender and the sauce has slightly reduced. Pour in the remaining 2 tablespoons of tequila and heat through for 2 minutes. Season to taste. Scatter over the pine nuts and a sprinkling of chives, and serve with basmati rice.

To flambé safely, toss the ingredients to the front of the pan, tilt the pan away from you and pour in the tequila. Light the tequila, shake the pan gently and leave until the flames go out.

Serves 4

3 tbsp pine nuts

4 tbsp sunflower oil

8 boneless, skinless chicken thighs

1 onion, sliced

2 garlic cloves, finely chopped

4 tbsp tequila

1 tbsp tomato purée

1 x 400g (14oz) tin chopped tomatoes

dash of Tabasco

1 tsp paprika

1 tsp sugar

300ml (½ pint) chicken stock

salt and freshly ground black pepper

snipped fresh chives, to garnish

steamed basmati rice, to serve

Acapulco Chicken

This idea was created from lots of leftover broken tortilla chips, and now it is a family favourite. Even friends request it when coming over for a casual supper! Use 1 teaspoon of chilli if you like it hot, 2 if you like it hot, hot, hot. Can you feel it?

Serves 4

1 tbsp vegetable oil

8 boneless, skinless chicken thighs, cut into chunks

1 onion, sliced

2 garlic cloves, chopped

1–2 tsp chilli powder, plus extra for sprinkling

1 x 400g (14oz) tin chopped tomatoes

175ml (6fl oz) chicken stock

1 x 400g (14oz) tin kidney beans, drained

½ tsp dried oregano

100g (4oz) tortilla chips

salt and freshly ground black pepper

soured cream and parsley sprigs, to garnish

cooked rice, to serve

Step one Heat the oil in a pan, add the chicken, onion and garlic and cook for about 5 minutes until golden. Add the chilli and stir-fry for 30 seconds, then add the tomatoes, stock, kidney beans and oregano; season with salt and pepper. Bring to the boil, cover and simmer for 20 minutes until the chicken is tender.

Step two Transfer the chicken to a serving dish and sprinkle over the tortilla chips. Top with a dollop of soured cream, some parsley sprigs and a sprinkling of chilli powder. Serve with rice.

Cheeky Chicken Tikka Masala

Forget having to wait for your take-away chicken tikka: this is one of the easiest curries there is to make. If it's summer, why not have a go at cooking the chicken skewers over the old barbie?

Step one Place the chicken breasts in a large bowl and mix with the ginger, garlic, chilli, salt, pepper, coriander, lime juice and 1 tablespoon of the oil. Set aside for 2 hours.

Step two Preheat the grill to high. Thread the chicken onto skewers and cook under the grill for 12 minutes or so, turning frequently until well browned.

Step three Meanwhile, heat the remaining oil in a large pan and cook the onion and chilli for 5–8 minutes until dark golden. Add the turmeric and cook for 30 seconds. Stir in the cream and cook gently for a couple of minutes.

Step four Slide the chicken off the skewers and stir into the creamy sauce. Simmer for 5 minutes or so until the chicken is cooked through. Check the seasoning, adding some lemon juice to taste, and serve with rice or naan. Garnish with coriander.

Serves 4

4 boneless, skinless chicken breasts, cubed

2.5cm (1in) piece of fresh root ginger, finely chopped

2 garlic cloves, finely chopped

1 tsp chilli powder

2 tbsp chopped fresh coriander

juice of 1 lime

2 tbsp vegetable oil

1 onion, finely chopped

1 red chilli, seeded and finely chopped

1 tsp ground turmeric

300ml (½ pint) double cream

juice of ½ lemon

salt and freshly ground black pepper

rice or naan, to serve

handful of fresh coriander leaves, to garnish

KITCHEN TABLE

For a video masterclass on how to chop an onion, go to www.mykitchentable.co.uk/videos/choppingonion

Madras Coconut, Chicken and Banana Curry

Moist, tender pieces of chicken in a rich almond, coconut and banana sauce – always a dinner winner in my house.

Serves 4

8 boneless, skinless chicken thighs, halved

1 tsp garam masala

1 tbsp vegetable oil

1 large onion, thinly sliced

2 tomatoes, roughly chopped

450ml (¾ pint) chicken stock

2 tbsp hot curry paste

150ml (¼ pint) double cream

50g (2oz) ground almonds

25g (1oz) desiccated coconut

2 large bananas

salt and freshly ground black pepper

boiled rice, to serve

2 tbsp roughly chopped fresh coriander, to garnish

1 lemon, cut into wedges, to serve

Step one Mix together the chicken pieces, garam masala and some salt and pepper. Heat the oil in a large pan, add the chicken and onion and cook for 10 minutes, stirring occasionally, until golden brown.

Step two Add the tomatoes and cook for 2 minutes until beginning to soften. Pour in the stock and stir in the curry paste. Bring to the boil and simmer for 10 minutes.

Step three Stir in the cream, almonds and coconut. Peel the bananas and cut into 2cm (¾in) thick slices. Add to the pan, season with salt and pepper to taste and simmer for 5 minutes until the bananas are just tender.

Step four Divide among four plates and serve each with boiled rice, a sprinkling of fresh coriander and a wedge of lemon for squeezing over.

Creamy Cardamom Chicken

This is a mildly spiced Persian dish of tender chicken in an almond and cream sauce. It is quick and easy to make, and reheats very well if you want to make it ahead of time.

Step one Mix the yoghurt with the cornflour and set to one side. Cut each of the chicken breasts into three or four chunky pieces. Lightly crush the cardamom pods so that the green husks split open, then remove all the little brownish-black seeds from inside. Grind these into a fine powder.

Step two Heat the oil and butter in a flameproof casserole dish, add the chicken and cook over a medium heat until lightly browned all over. Add the turmeric, cinnamon, coriander and ground cardamom seeds and cook for a further minute.

Step three Remove the pan from the heat and stir in the stock, grated ginger, lemon juice and the yoghurt mixture. Return the pan to the heat, bring to a simmer and leave to cook gently for 15 minutes until the chicken is tender. (You can now set the dish aside until later if you wish.)

Step four Mix the cream with the ground almonds, stir into the chicken and simmer for 2–3 minutes. Season to taste and serve, garnished with sprigs of coriander.

Serves 4

150ml (¼ pint) Greek yoghurt

½ tsp cornflour

4 large skinless chicken breasts

1½ tsp green cardamom pods

1 tbsp sunflower oil

25g (1oz) butter

½ tsp ground turmeric

½ tsp ground cinnamon

½ tsp ground coriander

150ml (¼ pint) chicken stock

4cm (1½ in) piece of fresh root ginger, finely grated

2 tbsp fresh lemon juice

150ml (¼ pint) double cream

75g (3oz) ground almonds

salt and freshly ground black pepper

coriander sprigs, to garnish

Chicken Brummie Balti, Alabama Style

On one of my trips to the USA, I paid a visit to Birmingham, Alabama and thought it might be fun to cook them our Birmingham's most famous dish – the balti. And boy, did they love it… I could probably run for mayor, it got that many votes of approval.

Serves 4

4 boneless, skinless chicken breasts, quartered

2 tbsp vegetable oil

½ tsp chilli powder

½ tsp ground turmeric

1 onion, finely chopped

4 garlic cloves, finely chopped

4cm (1½ in) piece of fresh root ginger, finely chopped

6 tomatoes, roughly chopped

150ml (¼ pint) chicken stock

4 tbsp balti curry paste

1 x 400g (14oz) tin chickpeas, drained

4 naan breads

2–3 tbsp double cream

2 tbsp chopped fresh coriander

lemon wedges, to serve

salt and freshly ground black pepper

Step one Brush the chicken with a little oil, then dust with chilli powder and turmeric, and season with salt and pepper. Cook in a large frying pan or over medium-hot coals for 3–4 minutes on each side until well browned.

Step two Meanwhile, heat the remaining oil in a balti pan or wok and stir-fry the chopped onion, garlic and ginger for 3–4 minutes until golden. Add the tomatoes and cook for a couple of minutes until they begin to soften, then stir in the stock, curry paste and chickpeas.

Step three Add the chicken pieces to the pan or wok and simmer for 5–8 minutes until the chicken is cooked through.

Step four Briefly warm the naan breads under a hot grill or over the barbecue. Stir the cream and coriander into the balti and check the seasoning. Divide among serving bowls and serve with lemon wedges and the warm naan.

Fast Fragrant Chicken Curry

There are lots of lovely curry pastes on the market, and when you combine them with a few additional spices and herbs the results can be really amazing. You don't have to stick to just one cut of chicken for this curry: try a mixture of thighs and breasts. If you have time, marinate the chicken for even longer than stated for a more succulent treat.

Step one Cut the chicken into bite-sized pieces and place in a shallow bowl. Add the curry paste and yoghurt and mix well. Cover and leave to marinate for as long as you like: 20 minutes is fine, but a couple of hours is perfect.

Step two Preheat the oven to 190°C/375°F/gas 5. Grind the coriander and cumin seeds in a pestle and mortar. Heat the olive oil in a large, ovenproof sauté pan, add the seeds and cook for a minute until aromatic, then add the onion, pepper and garlic. Cook over a medium heat for about 4 minutes until starting to soften. Mix in the chicken and its marinade, plus the tomatoes and chicken stock. Add the sugar, season well and bring to the boil. Transfer to the oven and cook for 20–25 minutes.

Step three Scatter over the coriander and serve with steamed basmati rice, mango chutney and warm naan breads.

Serves 4

4 skinless chicken breasts

3 tbsp medium-hot curry paste

4 rounded tbsp natural yoghurt

1 tsp coriander seeds

1 tsp cumin seeds

1 tbsp olive oil

1 large onion, sliced

1 red pepper, seeded and sliced

1 garlic clove, crushed

1 x 400g (14oz) tin chopped tomatoes

100ml (3½ fl oz) chicken stock

1 tsp sugar

2 tbsp roughly chopped fresh coriander

salt and freshly ground black pepper

steamed rice, chutney and naan breads, to serve

Lightning Coq au Vin

We all like a bit of coq au vin once in a while, and mine is well worth remembering, especially as it's ready to eat in lightning time, which is great as, traditionally, this dish is cooked over a long period.

Serves 4

4–5 tbsp olive oil

6 boneless, skinless chicken thighs, halved

1 tbsp plain flour

8 button onions, quartered

4 rashers smoked streaky bacon, cut into strips

100g (4oz) button mushrooms, quartered

1 garlic clove, crushed

2 tbsp brandy

300ml (½ pint) red wine

2 fresh thyme sprigs or ½ teaspoon dried thyme

1 tbsp tomato purée

750g (1lb 10oz) floury potatoes, diced

½ tsp cornflour

2 tbsp chopped fresh parsley

salt and freshly ground black pepper

Step one Heat 1 tablespoon of the oil in a large pan. Dust the chicken thighs with seasoned flour and cook in the pan for 1–2 minutes on each side. Add the onions and bacon and cook for 2–3 minutes, then add the mushrooms and garlic and stir-fry for a further 2 minutes until well browned.

Step two Pour over the brandy and carefully ignite. When the flames have subsided, pour in the red wine and bring to the boil. Add the thyme and tomato purée and simmer gently for 15 minutes until the chicken is cooked.

Step three Meanwhile, cook the diced potatoes in a large pan of boiling, salted water for 10–15 minutes until tender.

Step four Mix the cornflour to a smooth paste with a little water and stir into the red wine sauce. Return to the boil and cook for a minute or so, stirring until thickened; season to taste.

Step five Drain the potatoes and mash well. Stir in the remaining olive oil and the parsley; season to taste. Divide among the serving plates and spoon over the coq au vin. Serve immediately.

Roast Chicken with Crunchy Stuffing and Bacon Rolls

For the best results here, use breadcrumbs made from day-old bread.

Serves 4

1 x 1.75kg (4lb) chicken

1 small bunch fresh thyme

3 bay leaves

½ lemon

olive oil, for rubbing

75ml (3fl oz) white wine

1 tsp plain flour

300ml (½ pint) chicken stock

2–3 tbsp double cream

salt and freshly ground black pepper

for the stuffing rolls

15g (½ oz) butter

½ onion, chopped

1 small leek, trimmed and thinly sliced

1 small celery stick, thinly sliced

100g (4oz) thickly sliced smoked ham, finely chopped

50g (2oz) Gruyère or Cheddar, coarsely grated

75g (3oz) white breadcrumbs

½ tsp Dijon mustard

1½ tbsp beaten egg

100g (4oz) rindless streaky bacon

Step one Preheat the oven to 200°C/400°F/gas 6. Season the cavity of the chicken with salt and pepper, then push in the thyme, bay leaves and lemon. Rub the outside of the chicken with olive oil and season with salt and pepper. Put into a small roasting tin and roast for 20 minutes per 450g (1lb). Loosely cover with foil during cooking if it starts to get a bit too brown.

Step two Meanwhile, for the stuffing rolls, melt the butter in a pan, add the onion, leek and celery and fry gently for 5 minutes until soft but not browned. Transfer to a bowl and leave to cool. Add the ham, cheese, breadcrumbs and some seasoning and mix together. Beat the mustard with the egg and stir in.

Step three Divide the mixture into eight pieces and shape them into little barrels. Stretch each bacon rasher on a board with the back of a sharp knife, then cut across in half. Wrap one piece of bacon around each barrel of stuffing and put seam-side down into a lightly oiled shallow roasting tin. Roast alongside the chicken for the last 20–30 minutes until crisp.

Step four When the chicken is cooked, remove it from the oven, drain the cooking juices from the cavity into the roasting tin and put the bird onto a board. Cover with foil and leave somewhere warm for 10–15 minutes to allow the meat to relax.

Step five Skim off any fat from the surface of the cooking juices, place the roasting tin over a high heat and pour in the wine. Boil until reduced by half, rubbing the base of the tin with a wooden spoon to release all the caramelised juices. Stir in the flour, then the chicken stock and boil once more until the gravy has reduced. Stir in the cream and adjust the seasoning if necessary.

Step six Serve the chicken with the gravy and stuffing rolls.

Pot-roasted Chicken with Herby Garlic Butter

Pot-roasting is a great way to keep chicken succulent, and the bed of vegetables in the pot imparts loads of flavour. I like this with a dollop of creamy mash.

Serves 4

75g (3oz) unsalted butter, at room temperature

2 garlic cloves, crushed

2 tbsp chopped mixed fresh herbs (flat-leaf parsley, tarragon and basil)

1 tbsp olive oil

4 boneless corn-fed chicken breasts, skin on

1 small leek, trimmed and finely chopped

1 carrot

2 celery sticks, diced

leaves from 3 sprigs of fresh thyme

4 tbsp dry white wine

2 tbsp chicken stock

salt and freshly ground black pepper

mashed potatoes, to serve

Step one Preheat the oven to 160°C/325°F/gas 3. Place the butter in a food-processor with the garlic, chopped herbs and seasoning. Blend briefly and transfer to a small bowl using a spatula. Chill until needed.

Step two Heat a flameproof casserole dish over a medium-high heat. Add the oil, then add the chicken breasts, skin-side down. Cook for a few minutes on each side until golden brown. Transfer to a plate.

Step three Add the leek, carrot, celery and thyme to the casserole and sauté for about 5 minutes until just starting to soften but not colour. Pour in the wine and chicken stock and allow to bubble down a little, then arrange the chicken breasts on top. Cover with a lid and transfer to the oven to cook for another 20 minutes until the chicken is tender.

Step four Lift the cooked chicken breasts onto a warm plate. Whisk two-thirds of the herby garlic butter into the vegetable mixture and spoon onto warmed plates. Arrange the chicken breasts on top and place a scoop of the remaining butter on each one. Add the mash and serve at once.

Chicken Roulade with Cream Cheese, Chilli and Garlic

A really nice chicken dish that goes down well on special occasions. You can usually buy flattened breasts in your supermarket, or get your butcher to do it for you. For a special treat, why not use sun-blushed tomatoes in the sauce, in place of fresh tomatoes.

Step one Lay the chicken on a flat surface without the fillet (the extra flap of meat attached to the breast). Beat the cream cheese until smooth, then add the garlic, chilli, chives and a touch of seasoning. Spread over the breasts, leaving the edges clear. Lay the flattened fillet on top, then roll up, starting with the pointed end and turning the edges in so the filling is sealed in when cooking.

Step two Cut four pieces of foil about 15cm (6in) square. Brush with a little oil on the shiny side. Put one chicken 'sausage' on each sheet and roll the foil up tightly, twisting the ends firmly to form a tight cylinder. Place in a pan with enough boiling water to cover the sausages and poach for 15–20 minutes until cooked through. If you insert a skewer into the centre of a sausage, the skewer should be hot to touch when it is withdrawn. Switch off the heat and leave the sausages in the water while you make the sauce.

Step three Put the shallots into a pan with the white wine. Bring to the boil and reduce by three-quarters to leave a syrupy glaze. Whisk in the butter off the heat to make a creamy consistency. Add the tomato purée, basil and diced tomato or sun-blush tomatoes, and season to taste.

Step four Unwrap and discard the foil from the chicken and make one cut at an angle in each sausage. Spoon a little sauce onto the centre of each plate and lay the chicken pieces on top, slightly overlapping each other. Spoon over the remaining sauce and sprinkle with chives.

Serves 4

4 flattened boneless chicken breasts, including fillets

125g (4½ oz) full fat cream cheese

2 garlic cloves, crushed

1 red chilli, finely chopped

1 tsp snipped fresh chives

2 tbsp olive oil

2 shallots, finely chopped

120ml (4fl oz) white wine

50g (2oz) butter, at room temperature

½ tbsp tomato purée

1 tbsp chopped fresh basil

1 medium tomato, skinned, seeded and diced, or 5–6 sun-blush tomatoes, chopped

salt and freshly ground black pepper

snipped fresh chives, to garnish

Chicken and Gorgonzola Pockets with Roasted Asparagus

Creamier blue cheeses such as Gorgonzola – or Dolcelatte or Cashel Blue – are best for this dish.

Serves 4

4 x 100g (4oz) skinless chicken breasts

100g (4oz) Gorgonzola, cut into 4 even-sized pieces

12 fresh sage leaves

8 slices Parma ham (or you could use rindless streaky bacon)

2 tbsp olive oil

550g (1¼ lb) asparagus spears, trimmed

sea salt and freshly ground black pepper

Step one Preheat the oven to 180°C/350°F/gas 4. Starting at the thick side of each chicken breast, cut a deep horizontal pocket into each breast. Stuff with a piece of Gorgonzola. Lay three sage leaves on top of each breast, then wrap each one in two slices of Parma ham and tie with kitchen string or secure with a couple of wooden cocktail sticks. Season.

Step two Heat half the oil in a large ovenproof frying pan and fry the chicken for 1–2 minutes on each side until just seared.

Step three Meanwhile, toss the asparagus spears in the remaining oil. Scatter around the chicken parcels, then transfer the frying pan to the oven and roast for 8–10 minutes until cooked through and tender. Remove string or cocktail sticks and arrange on warmed plates to serve.

Oven-baked Chicken with Chorizo and Artichokes

This one-pot wonder gives loads of flavour for minimum effort and is guaranteed to wake up your taste buds. If you don't have a suitable casserole dish, use a large frying pan, then transfer the contents to a roasting tin and cover loosely with foil.

Step one Preheat the oven to 180°C/350°F/gas 4. Drain the oil from the jar of artichokes and add 1 tablespoon to a flameproof casserole dish. Add half the butter, then place on the hob to heat. Season the chicken breasts, add to the dish, skin-side down, and cook for 2–3 minutes until lightly browned. Turn over and cook for another minute or so. Transfer to a plate and set aside.

Step two Add another tablespoon of the artichoke oil to the dish with the remaining butter, then tip in the onion and garlic. Sauté for 2–3 minutes until softened but not coloured. Add the chorizo and rice and cook for another 2 minutes, stirring until the chorizo has begun to release its oil and all the rice grains are well coated.

Step three Pour the wine into the pan, stirring to combine, then add the stock and fold in the artichokes. Arrange the chicken on top, pushing the breasts down into the rice. Cover and bake for 35–40 minutes until all the liquid has been absorbed and the chicken and rice are cooked through and tender. Scatter over the parsley and serve.

Serves 4

1 x 300g (11oz) jar artichoke hearts in olive oil

25g (1oz) butter

4–6 boneless chicken breasts, skin on

1 large onion, finely chopped

2 garlic cloves, crushed

100g (4oz) chorizo sausage, sliced

350g (12oz) long grain rice

150ml (¼ pint) dry white wine

600ml (1 pint) chicken stock

leaves from ½ x 20g (¾oz) packet fresh flat-leaf parsley, roughly chopped

salt and freshly ground black pepper

Whole Roasted Tarragon Chicken and Vegetables with Pan Jus

A family meal all cooked in one large roasting tin – everyone is happy. The chicken requires no maintenance once in the oven, as the tarragon butter under the skin bastes the meat as it cooks, keeping it wonderfully succulent. I don't know if you've noticed Chantenay carrots in the supermarket or at your greengrocer's: they are small, sweet-tasting and require no preparation other than a quick rinse, which makes them ideal for this dish. If they are unavailable, use organic carrots cut into 5cm (2in) chunks. For an extra-sexy sauce, stir a teaspoon of Dijon mustard and 2 tablespoons of crème fraîche into the jus before serving.

Serves 4

50g (2oz) butter, at room temperature

1 garlic clove, crushed

2 tbsp chopped fresh tarragon

1 medium chicken

1 lemon

500g (1lb 2oz) medium-large new potatoes

250g (9oz) Chantenay carrots

2 tbsp olive oil

2 leeks, trimmed and cut into chunks

salt and freshly ground black pepper

Step one Place the butter, garlic and tarragon in a small bowl, add seasoning and mix together.

Step two Using your hands, and starting from the neck end of the bird, carefully loosen the skin around the chicken breasts. Spread the tarragon butter all over the breasts and pull the skin back down tightly. Half the lemon and put both pieces inside the cavity of the chicken. Place the bird in a large roasting tin.

Step three Preheat the oven to 200°C/400°F/gas 6. Wash the potatoes, cut them in half and parboil them in salted water for 5 minutes. Drain the potatoes and arrange around the chicken with the carrots. Drizzle over the oil, season and roast the chicken and vegetables on the middle shelf of the oven for 30 minutes.

Step four Add the leeks to the roasting tin, baste with the pan juices and roast for a further 30–40 minutes until the chicken is cooked and the veggies are tender.

Step five Carve the chicken into thick slices and serve with the roasted vegetables and with the pan juices poured over.

Seared Chicken with Guacamole, Tomato and Lime

I like to cook this chicken on a ridged griddle pan as it gives the chicken lovely markings and a wonderful smoky taste, but you can just as well use a non-stick frying pan. If time allows, leave the chicken to marinate in the lime mixture for an hour as it makes it incredibly tender. This chicken is also great stuffed into pitta pockets with some shredded lettuce.

Step one Heat a heavy-based ridged griddle pan or a large non-stick frying pan. Finely grate the zest from the lime and place in a bowl, then cut the lime in half and squeeze the juice from one half into the bowl. Cut the other half into four wedges and set aside.

Step two Add the olive oil to the lime mixture with half of the coriander, a pinch of salt and plenty of freshly ground black pepper. Rub the mixture over the chicken slices, then cook on the griddle pan for 4–5 minutes until cooked through and golden brown, turning once.

Step three Meanwhile, place the guacamole in a bowl and mix in the remaining coriander and the tomato. Season to taste.

Step four Arrange the griddled chicken slices on plates with a good dollop of the guacamole on the side. Squeeze over the lime wedges to serve.

Serves 4

1 lime

2 tbsp olive oil

2 tbsp chopped fresh coriander

4 x 100g (4oz) boneless, skinless chicken breasts, each cut into 6–7 slices

1 x 170g (5¾oz) tub of good-quality, shop-bought guacamole

1 plum tomato, seeded and diced

sea salt and freshly ground black pepper

Seared Chicken Fillets with Honey, Lemon and Paprika

This is a sweet, sticky glaze, which will add extra flavour to your chicken.

Serves 4

5 tbsp olive oil

4 tbsp clear honey

juice of 1 lemon

1 tsp paprika

4 x 100g (4oz) boneless, skinless chicken breasts

2 x 75g (3oz) packets mixed baby salad leaves

sea salt and freshly ground black pepper

Step one Place 2 tablespoons of the olive oil in a shallow, non-metallic dish and add 1 tablespoon of the honey, half the lemon juice and the paprika. Season to taste and stir together until well combined.

Step two Cut each chicken breast in half horizontally and add to the honey mixture. Stir until well coated, then set aside for at least 10 minutes, or up to 24 hours covered with cling film in the fridge, if time allows.

Step three Combine the remaining olive oil, honey and lemon juice, and season. Set the dressing aside.

Step four Heat a ridged griddle pan or large non-stick frying pan until smoking hot. Add the chicken pieces and sear for 1–2 minutes on each side until cooked through and lightly caramelised.

Step five Lightly coat the salad leaves with the dressing, pile them onto plates and arrange the griddled chicken pieces on top to serve.

Crisp Filo-wrapped Mustard Chicken

This is a great dish served with sprouting broccoli for low-fat entertaining. Crisp filo pastry surrounds the moist, tender chicken to seal in those lovely flavours. Traditionally, melted butter was spread between the layers of filo pastry, but by using oil from a sprayer this dish contains less than half the fat.

Step one Heat the oil in a large frying pan and fry the chicken for 4 minutes on each side until lightly golden.

Step two Mix together the marjoram, mustard, garlic and lemon zest; season generously. Spread the mustard mixture evenly over each chicken breast.

Step three Preheat the oven to 190°C/375°F/gas 5. Lay a sheet of filo pastry flat on a work surface and spray with a little oil, then top with another sheet of filo pastry. Lay 1 chicken breast in the centre of the pastry, lift the edges of the pastry over the chicken and scrunch it over the top to enclose. Repeat with the remaining filo pastry and mustard chicken breasts to make 4 parcels. Arrange on a baking sheet and bake for 20 minutes until crunchy and golden.

Step four Place the filo-wrapped chicken parcels on to warmed serving plates and serve with fresh, steamed sprouting broccoli.

Serves 4

2 tsp olive oil

4 x 75–100g (3–4oz) skinless, boneless chicken breasts

2 tsp fresh marjoram leaves, finely chopped

1 tbsp Dijon mustard

2 garlic cloves, crushed

finely grated zest of 1 lemon

8 sheets filo pastry

salt and freshly ground black pepper

oil, for spraying

Spicy Tandoori-style Chicken

This dish uses a spicy, yoghurt-based marinade, where the acidity of the yoghurt acts as a meat tenteriser. However, don't marinate for much longer than suggested or the meat will get too soft.

Serves 6

6 boneless, skinless chicken breasts

1 tsp salt

1 tsp cayenne pepper

4 tsp sweet paprika

juice of 1 small lemon

250ml (8fl oz) natural yoghurt

⅓ medium onion, chopped

2 garlic cloves, crushed

2.5cm (1in) piece of fresh root ginger, finely grated

1 tsp minced red chilli (from a jar)

1½ tsp ground cumin

1½ tsp ground coriander

oil, for drizzling

Step one Make three shallow diagonal slashes on the top of each chicken breast and put them into a baking dish. Sprinkle with the salt, cayenne, 2 teaspoons of the paprika and the lemon juice, mix well and leave for 20 minutes.

Step two Meanwhile, whizz the yoghurt, onion, garlic, ginger, minced red chilli, remaining paprika, cumin and coriander together in a blender until smooth.

Step three Drain the lemon juice from the chicken, pour over the yoghurt marinade and mix. Cover and chill for 2–4 hours.

Step four If using a charcoal barbecue, light it 30 minutes before you want to start cooking. If using a gas barbecue, light it 10 minutes beforehand. Alternatively, preheat the oven to 240°C/475°F/gas 9, or as high as your oven will go.

Step five Brush the bars of the barbecue with oil. Shake the excess marinade off the chicken pieces and cook over a medium heat for 7–8 minutes on each side until cooked through. If baking the chicken in the oven, place the chicken on a rack over a foil-lined roasting tin. Drizzle with oil and bake for 20 minutes, until cooked through.

KITCHEN TABLE

For more recipes from My Kitchen Table, sign up for our newsletter at www.mykitchentable.co.uk/newsletter

Lemon and Thyme Chicken with Grainy Mustard Butter

The simple marinade for the chicken does everything you could wish for: the lemon juice tenderises the meat, the thyme adds flavour and the oil helps to keep it moist.

Serves 6

6 boneless, skinless chicken breasts

8 tbsp olive oil

leaves from 3 large sprigs of fresh thyme

juice of 1 small lemon

3 limes, to serve

salt and freshly ground black pepper

for the mustard butter

50g (2oz) butter, at room temperature

finely grated zest of ½ small lemon

2 tbsp wholegrain mustard

leaves from 4 sprigs of fresh thyme

2 garlic cloves, crushed

leaves from 3 sprigs of fresh parsley, chopped

Step one Make three shallow diagonal slashes on the top of each chicken breast and put them into a baking dish. Add the olive oil, thyme, lemon juice, ½ teaspoon salt and some pepper, mix well and leave to marinate for at least 1 hour or overnight.

Step two Mix together the ingredients for the mustard butter with ¼ teaspoon salt and some black pepper. Set aside somewhere cool until needed.

Step three If using a charcoal barbecue, light it 30 minutes before you want to start cooking. If using a gas barbecue, light it 10 minutes beforehand. Alternatively, you can use a ridged griddle pan or frying pan, heating it until very hot.

Step four Brush the bars of the barbecue with oil. Shake the excess marinade off the chicken pieces and cook over a medium heat for 7–8 minutes on each side until cooked through. Serve dotted with the mustard butter and barbecued halves of lime.

Chicken, Leek and Potato Pot Pie

This is real comfort food, which I like to serve with some buttered broccoli or peas. You can replace the chicken with bite-sized pieces of salmon, which just need to be seared before folding them into the reduced cream sauce. Otherwise, try adding leftover cubes of cooked ham and/or roast chicken to the finished sauce.

Serves 4

6 boneless, skinless chicken thighs, cut into bite-sized pieces

2 tbsp olive oil

2 leeks, trimmed and sliced

350g (12oz) floury potatoes (e.g. Maris Piper or King Edward), peeled and cut into bite-sized pieces

300ml (½ pint) double cream

1 x 375g (13oz) pack ready-rolled puff pastry, thawed if frozen

sea salt and freshly ground black pepper

Step one Preheat the oven to 220°C/425°F/gas 7. Season the chicken pieces. Heat half the oil in a large heavy-based frying pan and add the chicken pieces, then fry over a medium heat until just sealed. Remove from the pan with a slotted spoon and set aside on a plate.

Step two Add the remaining oil to the frying pan, tip in the leeks and potatoes and fry over a medium heat for 5 minutes or until the leeks are soft and the potatoes are nicely coated. Return the chicken to the pan and pour over the cream (reserve a tablespoon for brushing the top of the pie). Bring to the boil, then reduce the heat and simmer for 3–4 minutes until the cream has slightly reduced and thickened and the potatoes are almost tender. Season to taste.

Step three Transfer the chicken and potato mixture to a 1.2 litre (2 pint) pie dish and allow to cool slightly. Meanwhile, roll out the ready-rolled pastry to cut a slightly larger round than the pie dish. Cut the trimmings into long thin strips about 2.5cm (1in) wide (but don't be too fussy). Dampen the rim of the pie dish with water, then line with the pastry strips. Brush with a little more water, then cover with the pastry lid. Press the edges firmly to seal, then trim the edges and flute with the back of a knife.

Step four Brush the top with the reserved tablespoon of cream (but not the sides, as this will stop the pastry from rising). Bake for 25–30 minutes until the pastry is golden brown and the filling is piping hot. Serve straight to the table and allow people to help themselves.

10 9 8 7 6 5 4 3 2 1

Published in 2012 by BBC Books, an imprint of Ebury
Publishing. A Random House Group company.

Recipes © Ainsley Harriott 2012
Book design © Woodlands Books Ltd 2012

All recipes contained in this book first appeared in *Ainsley's
Ultimate Barbecue Bible* (1997), *Meals in Minutes* (1998),
Gourmet Express (2000), *Gourmet Express 2* (2001), *Low-fat
Meals in Minutes* (2002), *All New Meals in Minutes* (2003),
Friends & Family Cookbook (2004), *Feel-Good Cookbook*
(2006), *Fresh and Fabulous Meals in Minutes* (2008) and *Just
Five Ingredients* (2009).

Ainsley Harriott has asserted his right to be identified as
the author of this Work in accordance with the Copyright,
Designs and Patents Act 1988

The Random House Group Limited Reg. No. 954009

A CIP catalogue record for this book is available from the
British Library

The Random House Group Limited supports The Forest
Stewardship Council (FSC®), the leading international
forest certification organisation. Our books carrying the
FSC label are printed on FSC® certified paper. FSC is the
only forest certification scheme endorsed by the leading
environmental organisations, including Greenpeace. Our
paper procurement policy can be found at
www.randomhouse.co.uk/environment

Addresses for companies within the Random House Group
can be found at www.randomhouse.co.uk

To buy books by your favourite authors and register for offers
visit www.randomhouse.co.uk

Printed and bound in the UK by Butler, Tanner and Dennis Ltd
Colour origination by AltaImage

Commissioning Editor: Muna Reyal
Project Editors: Caroline McArthur & Joe Cottington
Designer: Lucy Stephens
Photographer: William Reavell © Woodlands Books
Ltd 2012 (see also credits below)
Food Stylists: Maxine Clarke, Silvana Franco, Sarah
Ramsbottom, Vicky Musselman, Angela Nilsen, Lorna Brash,
Beth Heald, Annie Rigg, SPK, Mari Williams, Denise Smart
Prop stylist: Penny Markham, Helen Payne, Marian Price,
Malika, Victoria Allen, Wei Tang, Sue Rowlands
Copy Editor: Helena Caldon
Production: Rebecca Jones

Photography © Woodlands Books Ltd: pp6, 13, 26, 33, 45, 70,
73, 89, 90, 102, 105, 106, 121, 150, 169, 181, 182, 185, 190,
202 by Juliet Piddington; pp18, 22, 34, 54, 77, 78, 93, 94, 97,
125, 129, 142, 158, 162, 165, 166, 198 by Howard Shooter;
pp21, 37, 74, 85, 101, 130, 132, 134, 138, 141, 145, 154, 170 by
Gus Filgate; pp29, 31, 62, 113, 114, 193 by Francesca Yorke.
Photography © Dan Jones: pp65, 189, 197. Photography ©
Muir Vidler: p4.

ISBN: 9781849903974